The Closet's All Mine!

The Closet's
All Mine!

From a Seraphic Single

Dorothy Cummings

Liguori
LIGUORI, MISSOURI

Imprimi Potest: Thomas D. Picton, C.Ss.R.
Provincial, Denver Province, The Redemptorists

First published in Canada by Novalis
Publishing Office, 10 Lower Spadina Avenue, Suite 400
Toronto, Ontario, Canada M5V 2Z2

First published in the United States by Liguori Publications
1 Liguori Drive, Liguori, Missouri 63057
First American Edition 2010

Library of Congress Cataloging-in-Publication Data

Cummings, Dorothy.
   The closet's all mine! : from a seraphic single / Dorothy Cummings. — 1st
American ed.
      p. cm.
      ISBN 978-0-7648-1961-2
   1. Single people—Religious life. 2. Catholic women—Religious life. 3. Single
people—Conduct of life. 4. Single people—Sexual behavior. I. Title.
      BX2373.S55C86 2010
      248.8'4—dc22

2010014541

Liguori Publications, a nonprofit corporation, is an apostolate of the
Redemptorists. To learn more about the Redemptorists, visit Redemptorists.com.

Printed in the United States of America
14 13 12 11 10   5 4 3 2 1

This book is dedicated to

Kelly Bourke
and Seraphic Singles everywhere

Not only, then, is man capable of aesthetic liberation and
artistic creativity, but his first work of art is his own living.

Bernard Lonergan

❋ Table of Contents

❈ Preface

For over two years, they called me Seraphic Single.

When I sat down at my computer in November 2006 and began to write online about the Single Life, I had no idea where that life would lead me. Catholic, divorced and thirty-five years old, studying graduate theology in a city far from home, I had recently had a revelation. I wanted to share it with other Catholic women. The revelation was this: it was okay to be a single woman.

That this was a revelation might come as a surprise to the editors of both *Ms.* and *Cosmopolitan* magazines. The Single Life, to many people, means freedom, fun and sex without strings. But for sincerely Catholic women, as for women of most faiths, the state of "single blessedness" is something a lot more serious, a lot more real, than the sugary fantasies of *Sex and the City*. Unlike our more secular sisters, we are discouraged from dulling the pain of loneliness with shopping, alcohol and sexual sin.

Partnership is the norm of the secular world and, despite the sexual revolution, marriage is still presented to women as a glittering prize. And this is neither surprising nor wrong. Marriage is, as theologians have told us since ancient times, the natural end of the human person. (Consecrated celibacy, like that of monks and nuns, is a heroic sacrifice of that end.) And most women, despite the feminist revolution, still hanker for a man and a family of our very own. The 2007 self-help book *The Rules: Time-Tested Secrets for Capturing the Heart of Mr. Right* sold millions of copies.

I read *The Rules*. My friends read it. I constantly referenced it as I wrote about the Single Life. And yet the book offered no guarantee that any of us would find Mr. Right. The future was a complete mystery, and we were afraid that husband and babies would never be ours.

And yet there was a lot to love in the Single Life. My spiritual director advised me to see where God was working in my life right then, so I had a look. I saw that I had talents, interests, friends and family. I saw that I was living in an exciting city, with plenty of opportunities for travel and study. I reread St. Paul's conviction that the Single Life was a life he would wish for everyone, and I decided to take it seriously. I reflected that if one were called by God to remain single, whether temporarily or permanently, then one should be as cheerfully accepting of God's will as possible. I dubbed this option "Seraphic" ("angelic") and I optimistically named myself "Seraphic Single."

"*Not every woman who wants to get married gets married*," I wrote, and before I knew it, hundreds of readers across the English-speaking world were reading my blog, *Seraphic Singles*. Predominantly young and Catholic, readers found my essays and stories about being an unmarried, continent, church-going Catholic worth a daily visit. They wrote comments. They linked to my blog on their own blogs. They sent me e-mails telling their own Singles' stories and asking for advice. They wrote from the University of Notre Dame, from Harvard, from Oxford, from Aberdeen. They wrote from across the USA, from Canada, from Britain, Ireland, Australia, South Africa and the Philippines. I met some of them in person. I even traveled to Scotland to meet my British readers.

And there I fell in love.

When this book goes to press, I will no longer be Seraphic Single. At the age of thirty-eight, I got married. Finding Mr. Right should not have been a shock: had I not received an annulment from the Toronto Marriage Tribunal over ten years before? The possibility of marrying again had indeed for many years lurked in my mind. But falling so completely in love—and with a devout Catholic man my age, to boot—was a shock, all the same. And it seems a very funny cosmic joke that, having accepted God's will that I be Single, and, indeed, having written this book on the Single Life, God called me to Married Life after all.

Most Catholics do, in fact, get married. But before we do, we need reassurance that the life we live as Singles—however frustrating, lonely and poor at times—is a life worth living. I hope that this book will help Single Catholics feel more Seraphic about the way of life in which God has currently placed them.

INTRODUCTION ❋
What if he's not coming?

As I said in the Preface, not every woman who wants to get married *gets* married. This is the cold, hard fact from which many of us run. Similarly, not everyone who gets a divorce and an annulment receives that second chance. Or we blow that second chance. Sometimes, our prince doesn't come.

There are countless reasons why this prince might not arrive. Some are historical, such as most of the men leaving town for work, or the anti-marriage trend of the sexual revolution. Some have to do with our circumstances: we work in a mostly female environment, or in a profession dominated by gay men, or in a profession dominated by celibate men, such as priests and religious, or in a community where everyone else got married at twenty-two. Some have to do with our poor choices: we dated the wrong man for a decade and have finally dumped him or been dumped; we date only unmarriageable men; we are drinking alcoholics; we are using users; we are bad-tempered harridans that no one can stand to be around. Some have to do with personal tragedies: we are physically scarred, maimed or plain as a pan of milk; we are chronically ill; we are "old"; we have been irreparably slandered in our communities; we are big-boned, full-figured or just heavy women, and no matter what we do, we cannot lose the weight. That is why Prince Charming has not come.

Or maybe not. Maybe some of us are just "too picky." I hear this one a lot, especially from grumpy single men. But what I, and many other chronically single women, usually want is just a nice man whose looks we find attractive, who is intelligent and funny and faithful, who goes to church, who has a job that he enjoys and is proud of, and brings in enough income so that if we lose our jobs, or have a baby, we all won't be in a financial mess. I wrote this once on a website, and a poster wrote, "Wow, you're picky." So maybe these men don't exist anymore or were all snapped up when *they* were twenty-two.

Or maybe not that either. Maybe it is an insolvable mystery. Maybe, for some inscrutable reason of his own, God has decreed from eternity that many of my single friends and I will never find The Right Man. Maybe, in fact, we have been called to be *Single*.

I am a Roman Catholic, and for Catholics, being called by God to be *Single* doesn't mean that we have been given divine sanction to be *swinging* singles, living only for the moment and ourselves. It means that we must discern how we can serve God and neighbor as single women. Unfortunately, it also means putting up with a lot of disrespect and presuppositions from others, including other Catholics. Some people think that single women are selfish. Others think we are losers. What I hope to do with this book is give a lift to the thousands of single women who are gradually losing hope that they will ever get married (or married again), or who have decided to cut their losses and embrace the state of life God has placed them in.

Live Alone
and Like It

Single but Sustained

Although fundamentally disorganized, I am becoming a creature of habit, and my Sunday schedule is sacrosanct. In fact, I know that if I miss the 9:25 AM bus to Harvard Square on Sundays, I have hit organizational bottom. But today I caught the bus and went to the chocolate shop on Brattle Street for my weekly cup of hot chocolate. Getting a table is never guaranteed in that little shop, but today I had my pick. I wrote in my diary and admired the sun bouncing off the yellow trees and the old building on the corner. One wonderful thing about Boston and Cambridge is that they are so often sunny. Spring, fall and winter, the view from the chocolate shop is gorgeous. Today, maybe because I am thinking so much about enjoying being single, I noticed two or three handsome young men walking by. They were blond, fresh complexioned, well dressed—and about fourteen years younger than me. One nice thing about being a Seraphic Single is simply enjoying the beauty of young men and then getting on with whatever I am doing, without regret.

At 10:45 AM, I left the chocolate shop for Mass at St.

Paul's Catholic Church. The 11:00 AM Sunday "High" Mass is not just the engine of my week, it is my greatest solace. I am old-fashioned in my liturgical tastes, and in my sensitive opinion, St. Paul's gets things right. The church itself is a beautiful neo-Romanesque building, the homilies are pitched high, as befits the Catholic community of the University, the rubrics are obeyed, and the music—ah, the music. The music makes me misty with joy and gratitude. I feel that this beauty is a foretaste of heaven.

St. Paul's has a boys' choir school. My brothers went to a boys' choir school, so from childhood I have associated Sunday Mass with music written for men's and boys' voices, not just congregational singing. St. Paul's also has a Men's *Schola*, who supplement the boy sopranos and altos. All the musicians of St. Paul's appear to be consummate religious professionals: they know the difference between "concertizing" and supporting prayer through music. I notice, too, that the hymns chosen for congregational singing are usually classic hymns of thanksgiving.

It took me almost my entire first year in Boston to brave the coffee hour, but I was glad when I finally did. There are some very friendly people there, and they made me feel right at home. Now that I am an old hand, I like to meet newcomers myself, and introduce them to the doyen of coffee hour, a lawyer who likes to meet everyone. Today one of the newcomers, a handsome teaching fellow, asked for my e-mail address before I left. As a Seraphic Single, I am not going to get overly worked up about that. However, it was quite flattering, I must admit.

On my way to the southbound bus stop, I stopped in at the Harvard Bookstore. It was crowded, and even if I weren't worried about my budget, the long and winding queue before the cash registers would have discouraged me from buying anything. But I went to have a look at the handsome shelves of exciting shiny volumes of Western Philosophy anyway, and was overcome by an ocean wave of gratitude for my life of intellectual privilege.

Then, providing icing to this rich Sunday cake, I spotted one of my single women friends, and we walked to the bus stop together. Crucial to being a Seraphic Single is good conversation, especially with other women. Of course, reading is another form of conversation.

On Going to the Movies Alone

Going to movies is not politically neutral. My mother objected to my seeing *The Breakfast Club*, thinking it would teach me to disrespect parental authority. My friend Helen threw a temper tantrum when her parents wouldn't let us see *Prizzi's Honor*. But beyond parental censorship, which I have outgrown, there are the social politics of going to a movie alone. Apparently, it is a wild thing to do if you are a woman. My mother is not keen on the idea. To her it seems pathetic, lonely and asking for trouble. I think Mom's ideas stem from the days when dirty old men roamed theaters, looking for helpless young things to grope. In my years of going to movies alone, I have never met these creatures, just as I have never stumbled upon teenagers making out in the back rows.

The first movie I saw by myself was *Madeline,* who, you may recall, lived in an old house in Paris that was covered with vines, and went out with her schoolmates in two straight lines. This, of course, is a children's movie. Waiting in the queue, I fretted that the cinema staff would think I was pathetic, a twenty-something woman with no child going to see *Madeline*. But it was obvious that neither the ticket seller nor the ticket taker could have cared less. Their glazed eyes stayed unfocused. And I enjoyed the movie very much and giggled along with all the mothers and little girls.

The last movie I saw by myself was Hans-Christian Schmid's *Nach Fünf im Urwald*, which goes to show how sophisticated I have become. I didn't think twice about it. I took the northbound bus to Harvard Square and reveled in the dark and leafy walk through Harvard Yard to the Carpenter Center on Quincy Street. The Carpenter Center has an impressive spaceship-style walkway, which one has to ignore completely, for the real door is on the right side. The building serves as an art gallery, and one has to avoid the depressing contemporary art displays to find the stairs downstairs to the theater. Outside the theater stands a white curved desk where students pay $6, an incomparable bargain in Boston.

Last night ended the Hans-Christian Schmid festival. The audience seemed to be composed mostly of Germans and students of German. Some people sat by themselves. One of them was an East Asian woman I noticed one Sunday; she has beautiful waist-length, thick, straight black hair streaked with grey. She looks like an embodiment of Harvard glamour, which I admit is part of my enjoyment of movies at the Carpenter Center. But above all, of course, I enjoyed the movie itself, which was clever and funny and I hope has improved my German by osmosis.

On the Bitter Cold

I live in a big, battered duplex in a poor but honest neighborhood in Boston. When I saw photos of its sunny rooms on the Internet two summers ago, I fell in love. But as the ad said "male applicants preferred," it seemed unlikely that I would ever live here.

Further searches for a place were unsuccessful. Landladies prefer to see what you look like; telephone calls from foreign countries do not suffice. My generous father gave me airfare and, after a day of searching in the blazing heat, I found myself in the deliciously cool kitchen of the big, sunny, male-only second-and-third floor apartment. The kitchen was deceptively clean.

I was more in love than ever. I had seen the available rooms—a covered porch, a tiny office, a spacious bedroom with four large windows facing east. The shared kitchen was huge. The shared parlor featured a china cabinet. The shared bathroom was…livable. The rent was astonishingly cheap. But I had one nagging doubt: how did Jon and Ted, my potential housemates, feel about living with a woman?

Jon, burned by years in humanities departments, suspiciously asked, "What do you mean?"

I said, "Your ad said you preferred male applicants."

"Oh," said my housemate-to-be, relieved but embarrassed. "The house gets really cold in winter. It's kind of… um…not insulated, though I've been working on the attic…And we thought…Well, men can take cold better than women can."

This sounded absolutely mythical to me, so I just said, "Well, I'm from Canada."

"Oh, yeah, well then," replied Jon. By then he was desperate to fill the room. I moved shortly thereafter.

It was a beautiful autumn. Sun poured in through my windows. I sat on the covered porch in the mornings and drank my coffee. I dawdled over the Internet in my little office. And then winter hit.

The mercury plummeted to 15 degrees, 10 degrees, 5 degrees Fahrenheit. Goodbye to the porch. Goodbye to the office. Good-bye to the parlor, the only truly warm place in the house, for my housemate co-opts it annually as his winter bedroom. I took refuge in my sunny chamber, shivering beside the space heater. The four windows, now covered in thick plastic for insulation, still let in plenty of cold air with the light.

Cold! My waking thought every winter morning. At home with my indulgent parents, I turn the thermostat to a toasty 78 degrees. Here in Boston, I have no idea how cold it is indoors; I'm not sure I want to know. The space heater runs on money; the bill is enormous. I try not to use it. Like the Little Match Girl, I am in danger of burning all my capital on heat. I have pulled my clammy bed away from the wall and positioned it beside the fickle radiator. I climb into bed wearing pajamas over a sweatsuit, mismatched socks, sometimes a yellow terrycloth bathrobe. I lie immobile, thinking warm thoughts.

Temperature, says a physicist friend, is movement. Cold is just molecules moving slowly. Like a molecule, I move slowly all winter, slowly climbing out of my lukewarm bed, slowly moving to the frosty kitchen, slowly deciding to get out of the blessedly hot shower, slowly going out into the frigid Boston weather. I dream of Canada, of its thousand and one ways to beat the cold—insulation, heated tunnels, almost universal central heating—and of home.

Staying Seraphic

A fortysomething woman once asked me how you can stay seraphic when you are an older single and when it seems that marriage mightn't happen. I pondered this question while traveling; while my train roared and screamed across the countryside, I came up with a list.

1. **Remember that there is no better time in history and no better place than the West to be a single woman.** Life used to be very frightening and humiliating for all but the richest of unmarried women. In English society, unmarried women entered rooms behind married women: it showed unmarrieds' inferior rank. Nowadays, it is more difficult to tell married women from unmarried women, thanks to that "Ms." Remember also that this new Catholic obsession with marriage is exactly that: new. For over a thousand years, one form of single life—religious life—was believed to be superior.

2. **Accept that you will not be seraphic 100% of the time.** Don't beat yourself up for feeling bitter, sad and disappointed now and then. But don't beat up on anyone else either, and don't swim too long in your feelings. Take it up with God. Have it out by talking to the crucifix or writing God a letter. Tell him the truth: "Dear God, I'm very angry today. Another one of my friends is getting married, and although I'm happy she's happy, I feel …."

When you are done, ask God to take unwanted feelings away.

3. **Keep busy.** The good thing about a 9-to-5 job is that it keeps you busy from 9 to 5. Students and freelancers, of course, have a harder time fashioning comforting structures. I need help with this myself.

4. **Make plans with friends.** If you have no friends, this action is impossible, of course, and being single is not the worst of your problems. Keep in touch with old friends and stay open to making new ones.

5. **Make evening plans for yourself.** You could cozy up at home with a DVD or go out to a movie or a class. The advantage of taking a night class is that you might make new friends. Also, when you get home, you will be so tired, that empty bed will look beautiful.

6. **Socialize with married friends and relatives**—ones you truly like and who don't make you feel self-conscious about being single. Their dynamics will rub some of the glamour off the married life for you. Even the most loving of couples seem to bicker. "Now, Tom, *dear!*" "Now *Suzie!*" It's normal, natural and healthy, but it sure ain't fairy dust.

7. **Travel on a whim, even if it's just across town.** For me, that is one great plus about being single. I have the freedom to go where I want and, work permitting, when I want.

8. **If you can afford it, invest in your body beautiful.** Pick a beautician you can have a conversation with. Eat properly and try to get some exercise.

9. **Don't drink alcohol alone** (or at all, if you have a weakness in that direction). Invest in a variety of herbal teas instead. A little ice cream now and again won't hurt you.

10. **Invest for that little old lady in your future.** When you can, sock some savings away regularly somewhere they can grow. Take an interest in the youngest members of your family, so that they will think of Aunt or Cousin with fondness and gratitude. Consume calcium and do weight-bearing exercises. I once met a muscular old lady who was on her way to a mountain-climbing trip. I want to be that old lady.

11. **Remember that although one day you will be too old to give birth, you will never be too old to fall in love and get married.**

Laundry for One

At my undergraduate college, one of my professors was a confirmed old bachelor in the Oxbridge mould. His office was a mess of papers and books. A picture of the queen adorned one wall. When he showed us slides of classical ruins, his mother often appeared in the foreground. His ears stuck straight out of his head, and he was often caricatured in the student newspaper. He went to Latin Mass. It never occurred to me that he might be gay, and indeed I don't believe he is. He's a confirmed bachelor. Full stop.

Not long ago, a Toronto magazine did a short profile on this professor, and the interviewer asked him if he ever wished he were married. My professor said something like, "Well, it would be someone to help bring home the shopping."

I had a similar thought the other day when I was bringing home my laundry and fell on the stairs. Since I am only one person, you would expect me to have only a small load of laundry. However, my practice is not to do laundry until I have run out of clean clothes. This didn't used to take that long, but then a friend cleaned out her closet. Overnight my wardrobe quadrupled. Thus, the pile of laundry in the hockey bag by my radiator grew to a great height before I broke down, divided it into three piles, and lugged both hockey bag (which, mercifully, has wheels) and a bundle wrapped in sheets to the laundromat around the corner.

As it was the middle of the week and during the day, the laundromat was completely empty, which was a blessing. But I had the same quarrel I always have with the change machine.

"Eat the ten dollar bill," I tell the machine, making the edge as flat as possible. "You LIKE the ten dollar bill."

"Bzzzzzz" says the machine, sucking in the ten-dollar bill.

"Bzzzzzz" says the machine, spitting out the ten-dollar bill.

So, as often as not, I have to go to the sandwich shop next door to get the bill changed.

"Eat the five-dollar bill," I then tell the machine. "Look, Abraham Lincoln. Mmmm. Yummy."

"Bzzzz...Bzzzzzzzz."

"No, you LIKE Abraham Lincoln. Eat him."

"Bzzzzzz...Clankety clankety clankety clankety!"

This week my laundry filled four big machines. I folded up my clean clothes nicely on the spot and lugged them all back. The great thing about having the laundromat around the corner is that I can go home between loads and work. But with all that running back and forth, I was tired by the time I was climbing up the stairs with my burden and—*crunch*. I fell. At that moment I was decidedly against the Single Life. It's not that I want someone to help bring home the washing; it's that I want the combined purchasing power to buy my own washing machine.

The Grass Isn't Greener

I have a wicked headache and have had it since last night.
It may have started when I was called upon to mediate
between two nuns. Had I not been so tired, I would have
refused.

There are a number of reasons I have not become a religious. The first is that in my country, most of them abandoned
the habit and became invisible. At my convent high school,
the nuns who were left didn't look awesome or holy. To my
critical teenage eyes, they looked dowdy and old, dressed in
rayon and polyester. One sister, I am happy to say, did wear
marvelous sweaters and tweed suits, but her family "had
money," as we say, and the rumor was that they gave her the
beautiful clothes.

The second reason I did not pursue religious life is due
to a visit from the younger-than-average nun who spoke to
my twelfth-grade class about religious life while we were on
retreat. She was a plump, mannish, good-hearted, big-voiced
woman who embarrassed me. She clumsily shared that becoming a nun didn't mean you weren't still attracted to men.
When she saw a cute guy in the supermarket, she thought,
"WHOA!" She threw her arms in the air to illustrate.

Still, I was a very pious teenager, so eventually I mentioned the idea of joining the order to the convent porter.
But there was no encouragement other than a pamphlet put
anonymously in my locker a few weeks before graduation.

Off I went to university and got a nice boyfriend. There I also came across a retreat workshop for a group of women religious. The nuns were somewhere else, but on the lecture room floor was a great round mirror and some instructions. If I remember this correctly, the retreatants were supposed to look into the mirror and admire themselves as the handiwork of God or "the new stone" or some other feminist conceit. I was reminded of the old Brownie initiation ritual: "*Twist me and turn me and show me the elf, I looked in the mirror and there saw MYSELF.*" The sentimental, dated, pop psychological twaddle that has replaced classical spirituality is the third reason I did not join a religious order.

The fourth reason I did not pursue religious life is that I kept meeting angry, unpleasant nuns. Now, I have met some happy, very pleasant nuns, too, mostly from Europe and Asia. But I have met some truly bitter and biting North American nuns. One who stands out most strongly works for a factory and lives alone in an apartment. That, too—that strange redefinition of community life, was another barrier for me.

Finally, I was turned down sight unseen by the one order that caught my imagination in recent years. I was relaxing in my Boston kitchen, missing my girlfriends back home, when my eye fell on a glossy brochure featuring a photograph of young nuns in black-and-white habits. The brochure was part of a begging letter to my housemate Ted, and it encouraged Ted to send money to help this flourishing order build a new wing onto their convent. I examined the beaming faces of the young nuns and read about how this order had decided to cling to its traditional way of life amid the hurricanes of change following the Second Vatican Council. As a result of their stubborn refusal to get with the 1970s, contemporary young women now were flocking to the novitiate. The nuns gave their lives to study, teaching and prayer. That, I thought, was the way of life for me.

I telephoned the order's vocations mistress and was shocked by how young her voice sounded. I explained how and why I had become interested in her order and trotted out all my theological and Catholic credentials. But two things gave the vocations mistress pause: first, my great age of thirty-five, and second, the marriage I had entered in my twenties and subsequently had dissolved. The vocations mistress said she would have to consult other nuns, and then she would call me back.

After a week or so, the vocations mistress did call me back, and her verdict was that I would not make a suitable postulant. If I had been thirty-five and had never married, I might have had a chance. Or if I'd had an annulment but was only twenty-five, I might have had a chance. But thirty-five with a failed marriage…Her tone was apologetic but firm.

Of course, the real problem was that I had no vocation to her order. If I'd had one, I am sure burning desire would have driven me into her office to plead my case. Zeal would have inspired me to camp outside the convent in the rain. Passion would have led me to offer to peel the potatoes for a decade, to scrub the floors, to sleep on the mat. But, not having a vocation, I just grumbled weakly to my friends.

So consecrated life is not for me. And somehow yesterday I ended up mediating between two of my very favorite nuns, and all I can say is, the grass isn't greener on the nun side of the Single fence.

Privacy

A dear friend of mine, after years of pain, is at last leaving a toxic domestic situation. She has found a nice apartment in a sketchy (and therefore cheap) neighborhood. Delighted, I assembled boxes and offered moving help. Now she tells me that the landlord, a foreigner who claims to own substantial property, has both promised to send badly needed work her way and asked her out to dinner. I threw a fit. I looked up at the sky and demanded of the Lord, "Why? Why does this always happen to her?"

In case you are confused, landlords should not ask out tenants. Landlords have power over tenants, which is why there are so many laws protecting tenants, laws that landlords often ignore. For millennia, landlords have preyed upon their female tenants, especially poor female tenants. They have also evicted Irish cottagers and cleared the Highlands to make room for sheep. My own landlords have told gentlemen callers that my housemate and I were not home, pressured me into buying mutual funds from them, and let my house fall into such a state of dilapidation that a braver tenant was finally driven to phone City Hall. Landlords, who have power, should respect their tenants' boundaries. My landlord in Boston has a tendency to arrive unannounced to make sure we aren't harboring extra people. "Who's that?" he demands, pointing to the cleaning lady.

The evil of landlords aside, my friend has had to fight to assert her need for privacy. She has been told that privacy is bad, or High Victorian, or bourgeois or nonsensical. I have countered with long speeches about the good of privacy. Privacy is human. Privacy is necessary to our dignity. Privacy is necessary to our autonomy, a way of remembering that we are more than a cog in the public machine.

Privacy is perhaps even more necessary to women than to men: we do not strip or relieve ourselves in public. Privacy is what women who work outside the home have sacrificed: strangers and bosses invade our space, demand our attention, take our time. (A housewife outside the home is usually a customer, and therefore wields power that a mere employee does not have.) Privacy is something that women who have unrelated male housemates have sacrificed: we live in public. (My poor housemates! I am not a beautiful object in the mornings.) One Canadian bishop once defined Christians as people who shared everything but their beds. ("How selfish," complained the man I was seeing, the one I had to see the police about.) I suggest that healthy, generous women are women who give quite a lot, but never their privacy.

There are many ways to create this privacy, which today is so difficult to protect. A woman can choose her clothes carefully, so as not to expose her skin or shape. A woman can choose to forbid people from entering her home. A women can choose to keep one room of her house for her alone. A woman can choose not to be touched, or at least to carry herself in such a way that men are nervous of taking liberties. She can certainly choose to reserve her body to one man, the one man that she invites into the most private realm in her world. But that man had best be her husband because other men might not appreciate the implications of the invitation.

The sad thing is that we women now have to fight for our privacy. No matter how respectably dressed we are, no matter how quiet and modest of bearing, we have to fight off the importunities of strangers. Men to whom we are not introduced strike up impertinent conversations, and we do not know how to extricate ourselves. Men whom we gently reject or reprove turn ugly. Landlords, especially if they live with us, sometimes treat us as livestock, eyeing our potential worth. They are businesspeople, after all. Our home—our place of privacy—is their business.

Maintaining privacy is difficult, but it is well worth the fight. Fight for your privacy, my dear sister Singles. It is there that we find ourselves and prepare ourselves for our daily journey into the world in which we live and yet, as Christianity teaches, are not *of*.

Ten Great Things About Being Single

If I had to say what I like best about going home to Canada for a visit, it is making coffee for everyone in the house when I get up. When you live in a family, you have to think about things like that, and it's nice. However, here I am alone again, and so here is my list of ten great things about being single.

1. **St. Paul said singleness rocks.** No matter how family-centered your parish, no matter how many cutesy couples show up for weeks at a time to make Father happy he said he would marry them, you're living the state of life St. Paul said he wished for you. Think of that on Mother's Day when you have to clap for the ladies with children.

2. **You can make sudden, life-changing decisions without asking permission.** You can give up your office job to work with orphans, or you can give up the orphans to work in an office job. If God says "Jump," you can ask "How high?" without having to explain the "God said jump" part to an outraged spouse.

3. **You don't have to agonize over *Humanae Vitae*.** Is artificial birth control a grave moral evil or a much misunderstood blessed aid to the unitive and procreative aspects of marriage? Millions of married Catholics have to worry about this. You don't. *Yes!*

4. **You are much less likely to be nagged about anything.** But I'm not sure you're allowed to screen your mother's calls. Throw towels around with abandon, just because you can. Whee! Bury your socks in the sofa cushions. Frame a pizza box! Buy an incredibly smelly but lovable dog. Let the cat box go for another day or so.

5. **You don't *have* to pick up someone from the airport.** But you can if you want to, and that makes you a nice person.

6. **You don't have to adjust the bed to deal with two different body temperatures and/or preferences.** If you marry a European, you might have to give up blankets. Can you imagine giving up *blankets*? But even if you marry a North American, you might have to share the bed with a dozen stuffed animals. Or even dolls.

7. **You can do whatever you want in the kitchen, even if that is nothing.**

8. **You don't have to deal with anyone else's sexual fantasies.** The words "You want me to WHAT?" need never cross your mind. Sex-advice columns are enough to keep me unmarried forever. Throw in the *Humanae Vitae* worries, and I might stop dating completely.

9. **You get to pick all the movies.** Never will you have to endure a chick flick (if male) or Eddie Murphy (if female) just to make someone happy.

10. **You can let yourself go.** Have another doughnut. Mmm!

No Sex
in the City ☕

Sex and Shopping

The idea that being single is a divinely appointed vocation is a fairly recent appropriation of an ancient Christian value. Christian celibacy was not just a sign of the Kingdom, in which there will be no marriage, it was a liberation of one's body from service to the secular state. In his wonderful *The Body and Society*, historian Peter Brown observes that classical civilizations demanded that almost *all* their men and women marry and have babies. Your body was not your own: it belonged to your family, your city and your state. A woman who was not a pagan priestess (like the Vestal Virgins) and yet demanded to remain a virgin all her life was a revolutionary. As the Roman Empire became Christianized, and even before men and women fled to the deserts to become proto-monks and nuns, many women elected to stay unmarried, becoming sacred presences within their family's home.

Later, of course, most religious men and women who sought perfection through celibacy entered religious communities. Somehow, in the Catholic world, the vocations recognized by Church and state narrowed to the priesthood, the religious life and married life. Of course, there were some odd women out—such as anchoresses and the Beguines— who did not live according to a set Rule, but authorities were slightly worried by them. Once again, bachelors were seen as shirking their duties and spinsters were seen as a burden to their parents. The Protestant Reformation heralded an even greater valuation of marriage in the West, at least in Protestant states. And in the 1960s, of course, thousands of priests, monks and nuns abandoned their parishes and monasteries to get married or, in some cases, just to enjoy the 1960s.

That addition sounds snarky, yet I think we can all agree that our Western cultures are no longer striving for perfection but for having as good a time as possible. And the two most important aspects of that "good time" are sex and shopping. I worry that contemporary marriage or, rather, partnerhood, has those goods as its heart. Finding a partner is a kind of shopping, and partners combine their earnings to shop. Sex itself is a commodity, and at least one popular sex columnist compares a woman to a car: if she doesn't perform a certain act (once deemed illegal and considered demeaning to women) she is like a car without a standard feature and "should be returned to the lot." It seems to me that women are now expected to master a wide variety of sexual techniques for which prostitutes once charged extra. Are women wives or whores?

Christian marriage must be rescued from this worldview. In the meantime, Christian singles who remain faithful to their baptismal promises remain a sign of the Kingdom, in which there will be no marriage, no sex and no shopping. Yes, this is a lonely and disrespected way of life. Is there an openly celibate single man or woman in the West who has not been mocked and told he or she "just needs to get laid"? And even married Catholics, resentful of the privileges that vowed religious used to have, will bridle at the idea that single life has special merit. But there is a freedom in our way of life that no one can deny.

On Beds

I do not like my current bed. It is too big and too cold and too clammy. It has no frame and consists of a queen-size mattress on a slightly smaller base. It sits on my worn pine bedroom floor taking up too much space, like a man sprawling in his seat on the subway. When my third-floor neighbor marches up or down the stairs late at night, the bed shakes. This scared the heck out of me my first week in Boston. I worried that the bed might be possessed. It was left behind by the previous tenant, and my housemates hint that he had a varied and exotic selection of overnight guests. I don't care how much education I have—that still sounds like bed demon–attracting behavior to me.

I have piled any number of blankets on this bed, but still it will not warm up. My Blanket Cave technique seems to work only with single beds. Eventually I will remember to buy a hot water bottle. Wearing socks to bed definitely helps. But I think the next time I have enough money, I will buy a nice friendly little single bed with a virgin mattress. I love to go home and sleep in my little yellow metal bed and to stay in convents and seminaries with their narrow wooden beds. (In European seminaries, though, the bedding is confusing, consisting of a bottom sheet and a duvet with a removable cover. Give me my two sheets and seven blankets any night of the week.)

The hardest part of going to bed alone for me is not "the fires of concupiscence" (I am lucky there), but the loneliness and the cold. My friend Lily suggested I focus on sleeping in the arms of my guardian angel.

"Yes, but I don't think he or she is warm enough," I said doubtfully.

"Oh, but imagine him enfolding you in his great feathery wings."

The problem with that, though, is that angels are by definition incorporeal and yet not necessarily to be trusted in your bed, if you remember what St. Paul had to say about hats in church (1 Corinthians 11:10). And although I try to imagine that my guardian angel is a strapping, broad-shouldered dreamboat, whenever I think about angels, I imagine them as tiny points of light dancing on pins. That is one of the drawbacks of studying classical theology: I cannot help but think that angels are irresistibly drawn to pin cushions and that in every house with a housewife there is an angel jamboree.

So I will just have to wear heavy socks and offer up my loneliness for the Holy Souls in Purgatory until I get a single bed. Or, if it turns out that I am called to marriage after all, I hope I get a nice, slightly overweight husband who gives out heat like a radiator.

How Far Can You Go?

David Lodge wrote a novel called *How Far Can You Go*, and I couldn't finish it. It was too painful. He thought he was writing about a Catholic worldview that had vanished with Vatican II. Ha! He didn't know about the John Paul II Generation yet. The John Paul II Generation hit puberty, saw a world of skyrocketing abortion rates, HIV/AIDS, teens with herpes, Internet porn, sleazy songstresses, and the movie *Kids*, and asked, "What was so great about the sexual revolution again?" And there was JP2 saying, "You don't *have* to take your clothes off to have a good time," and we sighed with relief. JP2, we still love you.

Therefore, the perpetual Catholic kid question remains, and it haunts me even now in my thirties: *How far can you go?* Luckily for me, the fires have died down a bit, but they are still toasting my twentysomething friends, who occasionally ask me for advice. My answer is *I'm not sure*. And believe me, I read every chastity book I could get my hands on when I was twenty. The nearest I could get to a clear answer was "it is wrong if you are deliberately exciting yourself." Well, come on. What do you mean, *deliberately* exciting yourself? The way I remember it is as follows: he kisses me, I kiss him back, he kisses me, I kiss him back. This goes on for some time. And then the hand arrives. He puts his hand there. I take it off. He puts it there again. I take it off. Incidentally, it has been some time since all that has happened to me.

My buddy McKelvie is very suspicious of women today because he isn't sure that they will even bother with the old removal-of-the-hand routine. He is afraid they will all but ravish him. His ideal woman is someone who will slap him when he goes *too far*, whatever *too far* may be. His chastity will be safe. Her chastity will be safe. There will be no panicky rush to the confessional the next day. Thanks to McKelvie, I believe that there are still guys who expect to be and want to be stopped. And any guy who doesn't isn't the kind of guy I want to go out with anyway. I am a big fan of male chastity. St. Augustine is my homeboy.

My advice is to take it slow. If, on a first date, Mr. Charming swoops in for a kiss at the door (or the bus stop), don't brain him unless you hate him. Kiss him back, go in, lock the door, and call your friends. Woo-hoo! If, however, he lures you somewhere for an obvious makeout session, trot out "But Nice Girls don't make out on the first date!" If he truly likes *you*, and not just your nubile female flesh, he won't ditch you over this. If he *does* ditch you over it, good riddance. The only exception to this rule, as the nice policeman suggested to me at the end of my worst relationship ever, is the sociopath who will take this as an insult/challenge and push your boundaries obsessively for weeks or months. Thus, my other advice is that Nice Boys don't make you cry and wish you were dead.

Pure

Reflecting on the story of the "Woman Taken in Adultery," chastity advocate Dawn Eden lists the unchaste women mentioned in the Gospels and remarks that they were forgiven: "Well, we know Jesus forgave them at any rate. Whether anyone else did was another matter."

In sex-obsessed North America, whether you have had sex or not is a political issue. Canada's philosopher–prime minister Pierre Trudeau declared in 1967 that "The state has no place in the bedrooms of the nation." But it seems that everyone else has an opinion on what you have done there.

For Hollywood, virgins are hilarious. That a man can be a virgin at forty is deemed a joke worthy of an entire gross-out comedy. That a virgin woman, "the virgin Connie Swayle," could—even in 1987—be kidnapped for a human sacrifice was the joke that powered the movie *Dragnet*. And the hilarity extends to anyone in real life who has hassled a boy, girl, woman or man simply because they had never had genital sex and were willing to admit it.

But for many others, virginity is not funny. It is serious. In my Catholic Christian subculture, virginity is THE ideal for unmarried men and women both. Many Catholic men and women are haunted by their desires and infractions against the purity standard that they or their advisers derive from Church teachings. Are they pure enough? What if they do *this*? What if *that* was done to them? It wasn't their fault, but it feels like their fault…Can their sexual sins ever be erased? Are they really washed white in the blood of the Lamb? Can they ever *really* be pure?

In other cultures, male virginity is not very important, but female virginity is the bank vault of family honor. Some girls are murdered by their fathers or brothers not because they have had sex, but because those fathers and brothers suspect that they have. Sometimes the reporter covering the murder mentions that a posthumous medical examination showed that the girl was a virgin after all. And then I want to vomit because somebody obviously thought that this information made a difference to the case.

St. Augustine did not think that loss of a hymen necessitated loss of chastity. Responding to pagan taunts about the rape of virgin Christian women (who, unlike the pagan Lucretia, did not commit suicide), St. Augustine ruled that loss of chastity requires assent on the part of the person. Thus, a rape victim was still chaste. Imagine my surprise, then, when a Christian mom I knew told me about a Christian girl we both knew, who had once been raped and was afraid to tell her boyfriend. "Do you think he will forgive her?" asked the mom.

Today I am divorced, but I was a virgin on my wedding day. In a way, it was a pity, for my ex-husband would not have married me if I hadn't been one. It was a subject that obsessed him. Unlike other women, he told me, I *deserved* to wear a white wedding dress. And having had a good classical education, he dubbed me the "Parthenona," the title of the goddess Athena that honors her perpetual virginity. When I wrote that word just now, the Parthenon came to mind: cold, white, sterile, broken.

My ex-husband called me his "virgin bride" months after I had ceased to be one. And since ceasing to be a virgin had been, thanks to stupidity and misinformation, a horrible experience, I did not relish the nickname. It was dehumanizing. I hated it. I hated him. I hated the old books that had taught me that ignorance was innocence. I hated the pro-chastity speakers who promised me that, if I were a good girl, married sex would be unending delight. I was envious, deeply envious, of my merrily promiscuous friends, who at any rate enjoyed sex and were not forever bound to men who hurt them.

Men and women are not bars of Ivory soap. We are not a homogeneous material like gold. We are not action figures preserved in perfect, unblemished packaging. We are not, in fact, pure. We are people. We have histories. We are active and passive. We do things and things are done to us. Some of those things are sexual things. Some of them we choose, and some of them we do not choose. Apparently, almost all men have masturbated. Does that mean that all men are impure? Tainted goods? Unmarriageable? And apparently, most men and women in America have genital sex (willing, unwilling or semiwilling) before they marry. Was I, bleeding and hysterical, ontologically superior to them all? No. I reject that. My only boast is that I obeyed the law of God by choosing not to have sex before I was married. That's it. That is all I can look back upon without regret. I obeyed the law of God. The ointment on the fly.

So my point is this: chastity is neither what you haven't done nor what wasn't done to you. Chastity is what you are doing now. Chastity is your disposition of will to do what God has commanded: to treat sexuality as a precious gift of God and to love your neighbor—to whom this sexuality reaches out—as yourself. No one has any right to judge a person who has made a public commitment to chastity on their past sexual experience. No one *ever* has the right to cast the first stone.

Fight the Power

A gentleman and I yesterday had a lively conversation about that dear old donkey, male sexuality. We puzzled over how quickly feminism did a 180 on the subject. At one point, lesbian separatism was all the rage. Hairy legs. Alternative spellings for "women." Sexual harassment seminars. The end of office dating. (Ha!) Wanting to be judged for our minds, not for our bodies. And we hated porn. We HATED it. That was one thing all women, left, right, up, down, from the Catholic Women's League to Gay Teens for a Free Choice could agree on. Porn was bad.

And then suddenly something changed. I don't know if it was all the money Hugh Hefner gave NARAL, the U.S. pro-choice organization, or what, but suddenly porn became cool. Instead of lesbian separatism, there is lesbian togetherness as straight girls make out in front of straight boys at parties. More than legs get waxed. Women no longer spell the word w-o-m-y-n but b-i-t-c-h-e-s, at least for women with whom they disagree. There are "Stripping for Fitness" seminars. Sex went back to the office. We hope we'll be judged for our bodies if that gives us the edge we need to get ahead in business. And we pose for porn. Another law student is in the news for posing topless; she posed for *Playboy*. "Lawyers are boring," she said. "I wanted to do something *crazy*." Teenagers wear shirts that say "Porn star." *Girls Gone Wild* actually exists. I get two e-mails a day inviting me to be like Ron Jeremy. Once upon a time, I didn't know who he was. But now porn stars are household names.

What happened? How did we get from men-are-pigs to let's-make-porn? I think I know the answer. I think it's about power. Because some men are pigs, some women decided that all men were pigs. They located their piggishness in their sexuality. And when they realized how much power sexual images have over men/pigs, they decided to get that power for themselves.

Obviously, the current state of affairs is not good for anyone. It puts men at a disadvantage, and it makes them angry. It puts women in dangerous situations, and it makes them unnatural. As unfair as it was, there used to be a small prostitute class in contrast to the majority of respectable women. Now all of us respectable women can belong to the prostitute class, too. Yay! We can go to a reputable bookshop and buy a porn star's memoirs, *How to Make Love Like a Porn Star*, as if that is something we would ever want to do. We can buy portable stripper's poles and put on shows in our living rooms. We can read *Cosmo* online to learn to do things for free that an Atlantic City hooker would charge triple for. Isn't that great, girls? Isn't that *empowering*? We once dreamed of ending prostitution. What are we thinking now? *If you can't beat 'em, join 'em?*

Good men have always known how not to abuse the power they have. They are taught never to hit women, even when women hit them. (This is one reason it's abominable for a woman to hit a man; she assumes he can't hit back.) They share their earnings with their wives and never make them feel ashamed for it. They do not cheat, because they do not want to lose their beloved's trust. They do not coerce women into having sex, because they are disgusted by the idea of coercing women into having sex.

Good men love women and want to make them happy. They just don't always understand what women want, and sometimes they find what women want unreasonable. However, at the end of the day, good men want the women they love to be happy.

So now that women have rediscovered our sexual power, it would be nice if we learned how not to abuse it. We could resist dressing in the provocative fashions we see on television. We could refuse to flirt with male bosses to get ahead at work. We could ground our daughters for a month of Mondays when we overhear what they did on Friday to get the boys excited. We could stop flirting with men we don't want just to feel good about ourselves. We could refuse to treat men as if their natural attraction to women made them pigs.

Good women love men and want to make them happy. They just don't always understand what men want, and sometimes they find what men want unreasonable. However, at the end of the day, good women want the men they love to be happy.

Whenever I have any doubt about the existence of long-term effects of the first fall from grace, I think about the war between the sexes. I can think of no other explanation of why men and women do such horrible things to each other. The love between a man and a woman can be so beautiful. Why do we so often choose ugliness instead? Fight the power. Stop the war!

Bad Boys

This morning I am thinking about bad boys and why women find them attractive. There are a number of books on this subject, and men do go on about it. However, I will just give my own opinion, impoverished as it may be.

I have always maintained that a bad boy owes his success with women to a supreme confidence in himself. Women love men with confidence, be they good men or bad. Women also fall victim to a charming, impudent smile, that "you and I know better" smile that even small boys perfect. The principal bully of my elementary school had it: he could charm mothers and teachers with one flash of that smile, but all children knew that he was a thug.

Many women are also in awe of the success that comes from a permanent stance of looking out for "Number One." Little girls are dazzled by beautiful ballerinas and prima donnas of the music world who have achieved beauty and fame by constant attention to their own bodies or voices. Bad boys are the prima donnas of later life, only their focus is not their craft but their own sweet wills. They achieve freedom beyond most women's dreams, by constant attention to it.

Kind women are rooted to the ground: they have parents to please, sometimes children to care for, a place in the social world to carve out. I think they look with envy on the rule-breakers, the men who just do whatever they want. I think that kind women also labor under the misapprehension that because they would never treat a bad boy badly, their bad boy crushes would never treat *them* badly.

Ah yes, women are knocked almost senseless by acutely cruel treatment by bad boys. Nobody, they inwardly gasp, could be that cruel. But, oh yes. Yes, indeed. That's what makes these bad boys successful: blitzkriegs of cruelty or whatever it takes to get what they want. They follow this up, of course, with a charming smile to all other adult women. Sometimes they even try it on the women they have devastated. ("*What?*")

These, though, are only the bad boys who get noticed. There are also bad boys who simmer in secret resentment. They are not moral heroes; they just don't have the guts or brains to get what they want. These are the bad boys who claim that they treat women well, but maybe they should stop since women seem to want guys who treat them badly.

I find these men almost more frightening than the charmers. One can avoid charmers with iron self-discipline. But the guys who simmer impose themselves. They're two-bit, latent bullies instead of professional seducers. They're the ones who sulk when they make clumsy passes that are rebuffed. They turn ugly and hurl insults. They are passive-aggressive. They send long, boring, self-pitying e-mails.

These days, I thank God, I manage to avoid both kinds of bad boys. Sadly, they still plague my friends, and so I simmer with rage. I want the bad boys, particularly the passive-aggressive ones, to leave my friends alone. There are many good men in the world; one of them called me from Harvard last night. We had a good conversation full of laughter. It was a lovely antidote to the male bullying I have witnessed of late. I want good men for my friends; I want bad boys, as a breed, to become extinct.

Got Game?

Men were deceivers ever. Now don't any of you men get angry with me. That's not my claim: it's Shakespeare's. It's from *Much Ado About Nothing*:

> *Sigh no more, ladies,*
> *Sigh no more.*
> *Men were deceivers ever.*
> *One foot on sea and one on shore,*
> *To one thing constant never.*
> *Then sigh not so,*
> *But let them go,*
> *And be you blithe and bonny*
> *Converting all your sounds of woe*
> *Into hey-nonny-nonny.*

It would be nice to believe that all men have changed since Shakespeare's day, and in fact too many of us do believe that. But the more I think about it, the more Shakespeare's plays seem to have the authority of…well, not Scripture, but perhaps the early Church Fathers. Shakespeare knew the hearts of men and women, and Shakespeare told the truth. He even knew that women could hold their own with men in smarts and in wickedness. He knew women could be Portias and Lady Macbeths; he knew many were Cordelias. He knew others, sadly, to be Ophelias.

Some men still try to get women to have sex with them by any means necessary. Sometimes sex is just an itch they think they really, really need to scratch. Sometimes sex is conquest. There is a lurid little low-life on the Internet who brags in a quasieducated fashion about all the women he's seduced. My friend Clio told me about him, and I read his blog once. I skimmed it with horrified fascination until I felt nauseous. I asked Clio why on earth she would bother reading such scum, and she pointed out that it gave good insight into how men think. It taught her the concept of "Game," for example.

"Game," ladies, refers to mental tricks that men in the Pick-Up Artist (PUA) movement use to make you chase after them. It includes showering you with attention and then suddenly pulling away. The low-life says that this drives women crazy and encourages us to pursue the men themselves. This point strikes me as very plausible, because any woman who is pursued and then dropped wants to know "What happened?" and "What did I do?" She wants to be showered with attention. Everybody likes to feel special. To women who have been neglected by their parents, or by boys in general, it is as instantly addictive as crack. What happened? What happened? What happened?

What very well may have happened is "Game." It has happened to me. I was asked out to tea by a man I hadn't seen in ten years. Over the hotel tea, which he paid for, he seemed to lose his train of thought a few times. He told me that there was something about me that took his breath away. I had a kind of queenly reserve. Et cetera. He walked me to the subway, telling me that I made him nervous for some reason. Et cetera. And then he didn't call me. So guess what I did? Yes. I called him. *Suckered!*

The sexual revolution is one of the worst disasters ever to befall serious women. I am not sure what the suffragettes and feminists of the 1920s and 1930s would think if they were teleported to the streets of twenty-first–century New York, Chicago, Montreal or Toronto. Perhaps they would have thought they were in hell. Women's images are served up suggestively on the platters of advertising. Little girls dress in revealing clothing. Adult women wear t-shirts that read in gold *"This is what makes me hot."* Our cinemas offer a nonstop cascade of sex and sexual violence. And the papers are full of sexual information and opinion. George Michael's "I Want Your Sex" blares from strip joints onto the streets: "*Not everybody does it, but everybody SHOULD.*"

One of the most bizarre aspects of being a practicing Catholic today is that along with feeling guilty for past sexual sins, *we are made to feel guilty for not committing new ones.* I have found dating irreligious men such a nightmare that I will never do it again. Once upon a time, no man expected a respectable woman to have sex with him. Now, apparently, they are shocked when respectable women *won't*. After all, they've had sex on tap since they were kids. Dirty magazines. TV porn. Trips to strip clubs with their buddies. Sexually liberated women "responsibly" carrying condoms in their purses. "Responsible" parents warning them not to settle down "too young." And so pity the poor Catholic girl, who knows (or imagines) that if she won't take off her clothes and have sex with her boyfriend, there are a hundred girls who will. She almost believes, because society has told us so day in and day out since we were kids, that he *deserves* to have sex.

Well, take it from your Auntie Dottie: he doesn't. He has no right to your body, my dear Single reader. None. Zero. Time and time again, we hear the bad news about men and sex, and we just can't believe it. Sex for men is like food. It makes them feel good and sleepy. Then they forget all about it until they feel hungry for sex again. Oh yes, they may reminisce to other men, as if about a great restaurant meal, or try to recall a particularly delicious episode if it has been a while, but sex for a man is not the tremendous, tremulous act of self-gift (or self-immolation) it is for women.

I will make an exception: I think men who are truly in love, so in love that they feel like their hearts are made of glass that the beloved woman could crack with one disappointed or angry glance, might experience sex as a deeply meaningful act. These men are usually called husbands. But as for the rest: no. Forget it. At best, sex is a three-course meal at Flo's Diner, a feast they'll fake a husband's love to get.

Men like the blogging low-life I mentioned above also love to get something for nothing. And having sex with a man who doesn't give a damn about you—or has a kind of mild affection, as he might for a favorite bus driver or a neighbor's dog—is giving a whole lot for nothing. The woman is giving up her safety, for one thing, her protection against pregnancy, STDs, cervical cancer and, not least, her peace. Sacred prostitutes of ancient times may have prayed for countless lovers, but ordinary women do not. The ordinary woman just cannot take the rejection of her whole self, the self that included her ultimate gifts to her lover: her body, her privacy, her utter vulnerability. In Robertson Davies's *A Mixture of Frailties*, a worldly woman warns a younger woman that love affairs can coarsen a woman's personality. Her heart becomes calloused. And, let's face it, if a rejected woman tries to make her betrayer understand her anger and hurt, he often has no idea what she is on about. After all, it was just sex. Burp.

I like to say this, and I'll say it again: I don't believe in men's beautiful words. I believe only in diamond rings. If your boyfriend truly loves you, he will want to marry you. Of course, this is a much more unusual and stressful undertaking today than it was a hundred or even forty years ago. So if you're waiting for your boyfriends to declare their intentions, girls, you're just going to have to wait. But in the meantime, make *them* wait. You owe it not only to yourselves but to the great host of women who are tempted over and over again to betray themselves because "everybody's doing it." Everybody's not doing it. Hang in there.

A Catholic's Rules for Dating

By now, the male reader may have given up in disgust. I hope not. Take heart, male readers! Herewith follows advice for both women and men.

1. **Know yourself**. If your *primary identity* is that you are Catholic, date only Catholics. And not just any Catholic, settling only for the cultural stuff—hold out for one who goes to Mass regularly. If you are striving to love the Lord your God with all your heart, with all your soul and with all your strength, you will not be happy with someone who doesn't share this goal. Apart from that, don't have a huge laundry list of what the perfect man or woman for you should be like. Pick *two* essential qualities, and then date whomever you like who seems to have these two qualities. Don't reject a nice person on a first or even second date just because they seem nervous and nerdy. They might just need to relax in order to shine. But do pay attention to what they say because, in my experience, the red flags (e.g. "I have a drinking problem") are waved on the first date.

2. **Be consistent.** If you are traditional and want to date other traditional people, be consistent. For women this may mean not asking men out on dates, at least not in an obvious way, and keeping in mind that traditional marriage means a lot of work for you. Being traditional is not a pass to perpetual princess behavior. For men this means getting up the courage to ask girls out, picking up the check and behaving themselves.

3. **Be just.** Like Sister Wilfreda told me in high school, don't date someone you *know* you could never marry. Don't waste their time to be "kind." And don't keep cuddling with them!

4. **Be careful.** In the early weeks of dating, a woman shouldn't go to a man's home or be completely alone with him in hers, especially not on the First or the Third Date. Exceptions can be made, but be careful, be careful, be careful.

5. **Be chaste.** Clothes must stay on. Any attempt on the bra clasp should be punished or at very least firmly and finally resisted. Don't make out on the first date; it sends the wrong message. Incidentally, ladies, an amateur kisser is more to be trusted than an expert. And he'll improve.

6. **Keep your spiritual director or confessor in the loop.** Dating brings a lot of unsettling emotions and temptations, so it is good to tell your professional soul-minder what is going on.

7. **Be loyal.** People hate it when their friends neglect them for their new romance. And people need their friends around them so that they don't do anything dumb, like get too attached too quickly. But be loyal also to your sweetie. Be careful not to betray his or her confidences to your friends.

8. **Listen to your friends.** They mirror what is happening to you. If your friends are virtuous people, and they don't like your new sweetie, there is probably a good reason for that. Ask them what it is. Friends are happy when you are happy and sad when you are sad. If you have to ask, "Why aren't you happy for me?" the answer very well may be, "Because you are not happy yourself."

9. **Be brave.** Don't allow your boyfriend or girlfriend to make you feel terrible. Stand up for yourself and what you love, and if your not-so-sweet sweetie persists in making you feel miserable, dump him or her. ASAP.

10. **Pray that God's loving will be done.** Love may mean marriage, but marriage doesn't necessarily mean love. A guy friend once told me, "If he/she really loves you, he/she wants to marry you." Sweet, eh? And maybe so. But it doesn't necessarily work the other way around. In my unhappy experience, wanting to marry you is not proof that a person loves you. Someone might want to marry you having convinced him/herself that you are someone completely different, the person he/she *really* wants.

Someone might want to marry you out of masochistic pity. Someone might want to marry you because they have hit a milestone birthday and are panicking. Either way, if dating talk is leading to marriage talk, *pray a lot*. Talk to your sweetie about all your thorny issues and fears and the insights that came up while praying. Say to God, "Thy will be done," and mean it.

Finally, always remember that God wants you to be *happy*. Don't date someone because you think you should; date him because you want to.

Men Are
the Caffeine
in the Cappuccino of Life

The Truth About Men

Today I received an e-mail from my friend Boston Girl, a tradition-loving, straight-talking, beer-drinking, book-learning, churchgoing gal like me. She was expressing her frustration that the man she had a crush on turned out to be twitchy and completely self-absorbed. To add insult to injury, he smugly hinted that she had thrown herself at him when last they had a drink together. What a jerk. My pal rightly faked confusion and made it clear she didn't know what he was talking about. Then she said she had to go and went.

She seemed to be asking for advice, so I gave the best advice I know about men, something that took thirty-five years to get through my head, and it is this: *men are who they are and not who you want them to be.* I wish I had known this at eighteen; I would have been saved a lot of sorrow and stupidity. Sometimes you have to look beyond a man's words (not to mention his handsome face) to see what he is truly like, but very often a man will tell you right up front what his faults are. I have dated an alcoholic who told me on our first date that he had a drinking problem. I thought, "Oh, he's my age, so he can't be an alcoholic. He must be exaggerating."

(Ha.) I have dated men long after discovering that they were atheists. I have thought, "Well, St. Monica turned her atheist husband around eventually." (Double ha.) The Canadian theologian Bernard Lonergan would call these examples of "the flight from understanding."

The second piece of advice I would give to a Single-But-Searching friend is to *pay attention to how she* really *feels around a man she is interested in*. If, after he is out of sight, she feels peaceful and happy, that is a very good sign. If she feels drunk and giggly, she should be careful that infatuation does not cloud her reason. And if she feels discontented, depressed or dislike for herself, she should wash that man, as they say, right out of her hair. When I think of the times I have called men who alarmed me just because I was pleased they liked me, I could kick myself.

That leads to my third piece of advice, the old ancient Greek classic: *gnothi seauton*, or "know thyself." When you are a young woman, it makes sense to meet and date all kinds of men, with the caveat that they must treat you with respect, of course. You haven't figured out who you are yet, and you can learn interesting things from different people. (Through dating, my mother learned about motorcycles and Studebaker cars and also improved her German.) However, once you have seriously moved into (post-school) adult life, you should have *some idea of what you do not want in a man and the backbone not to date men who have it*. You should also have an idea of what you can put up with, because no man on this earth is perfect. For example, even though I cannot stand men who are contemptuous of others, I do not mind men who are smug. And although I don't like men who talk too much, I do like men who don't talk enough.

"Maybe I'm Too Smart"

Teachers in my all-girls' high school reminded us of how lucky we were. In coed schools, some girls pretended to be dumb to make boys like them. There were no boys around—unless you counted two married male teachers, the janitors and old Father Sheehan—so there was no point whatsoever in us pretending to be dumb. In my not-so-Seraphic days, I sometimes wondered if I were single because I was "too smart." There is a rumor that men don't like women who are smarter than they are. Today I don't believe that this is true of all men, or even of most men—at least not of most men in North America, where I have spent most of my time. But one thing I have discovered is that men don't like women who make them feel dumb. Women do this most easily by looking at men with a "gosh, you're dumb" expression or making "Boys are stupid; let's throw rocks at them" jokes. This makes men *fume*. Of course, there is the kind of man who thinks a woman is intentionally making him feel dumb just by making a better argument than his, but a smart woman wouldn't want to date such an insecure fellow anyway. And I believe that most good men are proud of the intellectual accomplishments of the women they love and/or admire.

That said, I think women care more than men do about having a spouse who is at least their intellectual equal. I used to pride myself on dating only university graduates. But to tell the truth, my sweetest boyfriend never finished his degree. I was still in high school when I met him, and I thought that because he was in university, he had to be smart. Well, the poor boy was religious, kind, good and nice to his mother, but he was not very smart. Today he makes oodles of cash. But he is not now, nor was he then, an intellectual. And I have been, for better and worse, an intellectual since I won the fourth-grade spelling bee. One evening, after I excitedly explained a theory to a group of friends, my boyfriend's brother turned to him and asked, "Do *you* understand what she's talking about?" And my poor dear boyfriend said, "I just nod and smile." My blood froze. Reader, I did not marry him.

I think the best policy for my Single-But-Searching friends is to let their intellectual lights shine as brightly as they can. This will eliminate the few immature men who are frightened by brainy women and attract men who actually do envision conversations about phenomenology over the breakfast table. Meanwhile, we should all be careful not to sound arrogant or condescending to anyone and—very important—not to be impressed by arrogant intellectual men who condescend to us. An intellectual jerk is still a jerk.

Let Us Now Praise Good Men

When I was an angry young thing, still shell-shocked after my sad marriage and still adding to my collection of Andrea Dworkin tomes, I believed the worst about men. One cranky day, I wrote out all my beliefs about men. These included that most men hated women and that most men would rape women if they could get away with it. But then, after writing my list, I realized that I did not *know* if these things were true. They just *felt* true. So I wrote down a list of counter-statements. I wrote that most men love women and that most men were horrified by rape. After all, they were the ones who wrote laws against rape in the first place. And after finishing this second list, I realized that it was probably more true than the first. This was the beginning of my recovery.

Let us all now praise good men. I don't mean the usual heroes—Gandhi and Martin Luther King, Jr., and other famous men who did good to strangers but neglected or wronged their wives. I mean men who are good sons, good brothers, good fathers, good uncles, good boyfriends, good husbands or good priests to the women in their lives. I mean men who honor and respect women and show it in a thousand little ways. I mean men who are grateful for their mother's care, who are gentle with their sisters, who are a source of security for their daughters, who are trustworthy mentors for their nieces, who are fun companions for their girlfriends, who are the mainstays of their wives and who are the humble helpers of women who seek to know God. And thanks be to God, I know many men like these.

Women sometimes shoot themselves in the foot by complaining about men around men. They tell anti-man jokes at work, and thus make men resentful. My suggestion is to never complain about a man without mentioning a real-life model of male virtue. That way, men who overhear begin to understand what women think worthy of praise. Do mothers still cajole sons into eating their vegetables by promising that in so doing they will become big, strong men like their fathers? I am suggesting something on similar lines. Imagine if instead of saying, "Men are pigs," women were always specific about what was bothering them. For example, a woman might say to friends, "I wish I had a boyfriend who didn't always stare at other women. My brother has eyes only for his girlfriend when they are together." See the difference? It is the behavior, not men in general, that is condemned. What is more, the good behavior is presented and praised.

The good men will repay us for our appreciation of their goodness; I am sure of that. After reading about an honor killing in Ontario, I e-mailed my brother and thanked him for being a good brother. I praised him for never threatening me or harming me for dating or divorcing or any other behavior that, in some families, would get me killed. And he replied that, when the subject of women comes up, he often tells his coworkers how proud he is of his ambitious sisters. And I thought, his coworkers may be learning from that. Isn't that great?

Caffeine

A small controversy has brewed up over my favorite motto (invented on my blog *Seraphic Singles*): "Men are the caffeine in the cappuccino of life." Somebody grumbled, "Why not something more nutritious?" Now, this surprised me because I am an inveterate coffee drinker, and I thought that my motto was a grand compliment.

I sometimes wonder if men have any idea why many women are tempted to hate them. Really hate them. Hate them with deep loathing. Hate them with great overflowing wells of disgust. Small boys fry ants with magnifying glasses and blow up frogs. Older boys, unless they have been trained not to, play cruel tricks on alley cats. In my elementary school, the boys in my class had a game where they picked one of the "popular girls" and all piled on top of her, groping what they could grope. (When I finally complained to the principal, he replied, "Boys will be boys" and "This is all part of growing up.") Those same boys plotted to beat the hell out of me if I were allowed to join their hockey team. A younger girl confessed to me that she had been molested by a man in the street on her way to school. Another girl, a fourteen-year-old foster child, told me that she had an eighteen-year-old boyfriend, by whom she had been pregnant. She was angry that Catholic Children's Aid wouldn't pay for her to go on the Pill. When I was twelve or so, I picked up pornography that blew out down the main street. And all that took place in a quiet, wealthy, relatively peaceful Canadian city in the 1980s. Consider some places in Africa, where soldiers consider it a good joke to force boys to rape their mothers and to force fathers to rape their daughters.

Shall we go on? Let's not. We all know the horror stories. Women shiver over them. Men, as Camille Paglia has pointed out, have written law codes punishing them. Shakespeare said, "The evil that men do lives after them; the good is oft interred with their bones." I prefer to concentrate on the good stuff. As I told my therapist, I love my dad and my brothers. She, of course, was convinced I secretly hated my father and brothers. But, being seriously burned by marriage and the dumb relationships I got into to make up for it, I insisted, "No, I hate all men *except* my father and brothers."

That wasn't really true then, and it certainly isn't true now. I don't hate men. Indeed, I find them very interesting and usually quite likeable. One of the many benefits of theology school was being around men who were not interested in exploiting women, or in pursuing women, or in finding comfort and enjoyment in women's arms at all. I could relax. Yes, there were still some heart-burnings, and some of us girls trooped off to Father Rector to complain about this man or that, but I met some truly stellar men. Some of these stellar men, by the way, are married, so I'm not idolizing celibates here. And I've met seminarians who were jerks. It's just that it is nice to know men for whom all women are, and should be, sisters and daughters.

There are two extremes that Single women like me can fall into regarding men. The more traditional one is to believe that my life is incomplete without a man in it. Indeed, that is what Anglo-Saxon culture has taught since the Reformation, and what the Anglo-Saxons believed before Gregory the Great decided to send missionaries to convert them. (Catholic culture has always given women the option of communal female life in religious orders.) I could tear my hair—or rather have it straightened—and strive with might and main to be attractive to the Lords of Creation so that—please God—one might deign to marry me. As the t-shirt of one of the groped "popular girls" read, "You're no bunny till some bunny loves you." The less traditional extreme is to become a man-hater, full stop. However, I have long held that it is pointless for a traditionalist heterosexual Catholic woman to behave like a lesbian separatist. I mean, come on, who am I trying to kid here?

So here is my balanced position. Life, if prepared well, is fantastic. It is a great cup of cappuccino made by a conscientious barista on an expensive Italian machine. It must have hot espresso coffee, it must have hot milk, and it must have milk foam. Cinnamon and chocolate sprinkled on top are a plus. The espresso may be caffeinated or decaffeinated. However, there is something amiss with a decaffeinated cappuccino. It lacks zip. It lacks that certain extra something. And my life lacks that certain extra something if there are no men around. I *like* to have men around. So, gentlemen, when I say that you are the caffeine in the cappuccino of life, I am being chivalrous in my own way. I don't *need* you in a personal capacity, but I do *like* you. Let us all be good friends.

Max

1

It's a frosty morning in Boston, and what better way to warm up than to send my thoughts through space and time to a blazing June day in a bustling German city? It was on that day that, because I wanted to go to one of the city's famous trance clubs, my seminarian pal Stefan whipped out his phone and speed-dialed a young man I'll call Max. Max was apparently an expert on the local club scene. He was also available for lunch, so my seminarian pal and I went to meet him outside McDonald's in the main shopping district. Max was late. Stefan sighed with annoyance. And then—dark hair carefully gelled and mussed, shirt chosen from the clubbing section of a department store, yellow sunglasses turning his blue eyes green, Max arrived.

By now you may have observed that I am a susceptible woman. Despite being a Seraphic Single, I am the first to admit that men are the caffeine in the *Milchkaffee* of life.

But rarely have I fallen as hard for someone as quickly as I fell for Max. Over lunch I perceived that he was handsome and quiet, perhaps a bit shy about his English. After lunch, when Stefan commended me to Max's care, Max did his best to entertain me, which he did by imitating the English soccer louts who had invaded the city. ("*Tik-KUTS? We doan need no Tik-KUTS!*") When our bus driver refused to go any farther, blocked by the throngs of soccer fans outside, we alighted and continued on our way to Max's college (my residence) by foot. No longer quiet, Max chatted and joked and took my photograph. My head was quite turned by his attention. This all seemed almost ridiculous: what was I, Dorothy, age thirty-five, doing wandering through town with this intensely handsome creature, age …twenty-seven? twenty-eight? twenty-two? I couldn't tell. And when he asked me my age, I refused to say.

A few days later, as dusk fell upon the downtown, Stefan and I met Max again. We went to a restaurant and then to a club. In that city, the clubs don't close before 5 AM, and this one was still dead. To help the time pass, we all drank American-style cocktails, over which Max choked, "*Stark!*" As we sat there, waiting and getting drunk, I became more and more enamored of the handsome Max. The club filled up, and the dance floor did nothing to cure me. I was smug with worldly joy: I was in *Germany*, dancing in a German *club* with a handsome *German*! Never mind the looming Theology Department German Exam. This was *living*!

The next day, I was dying. I dragged my footsore, head-achy, hungover self into the woods behind the college. But I was blissfully happy. My body was positively buzzing. I sat in a meadow and plucked at grass, giggling uncontrollably. I was, I knew, in a completely irrational state of infatuation before which I was helpless. I was sure it would pass, but in the meantime, I decided to enjoy it and see what happened.

2

What could be less Seraphic than a doomed crush on a much younger German charmer with a short attention span?

I spent much of the summer in a state of acute self-consciousness. First of all, I was thirty-five in a world of twentysomethings who kept asking me my age. Second, my German was rudimentary, and whether my interlocutor was fluent in English, faked how much English he understood, or smiled in an embarrassed, uncomprehending way, I felt like an English-language imperialist. Third, my ancestors and their friends had a habit of going to Germany and dropping bombs on it. The cheerful remark "I'm from Dresden" threw me into guilt-tinged gloom. So my nerves did not need Max to direct his blue-eyed gaze upon me, dazzle me with his thousand-watt smile, confound me with saucy remarks and disappear into the rest of his life for days on end.

Strange as this may sound, I myself was the possessor of some glamour, which is probably why Max paid any attention to me at all. I was a foreign woman with an exotic American address and yet the (contemporary, relative) innocence of Canadian citizenship. I was a doctoral student and so, in this highly organized society, outranked all the undergrads. I was an older woman ("Maybe twenty-six?"), which was not the mortal sin it is in North America. Finally, I kept telling Germans that knowledge of German is crucial to graduate studies in theology, which made them all happy.

Interestingly, the theological German I already knew did not square with Max. In both Canada and the USA, my professors refer, half-jokingly, to their thesis directors as their *Doktorvaters*. Max was profoundly shocked to hear this expression and said that it was most politically incorrect. We righted the injustice by "inventing" the word *Doktormutter*. I lived to regret it, for Max called me *Doktormutter* ever after. This made me feel old, and it made Max's outrageous flirtation almost unbearably cheeky. At an otherwise civilized college banquet, I found myself saddled with an enormous plate of meat as Max loudly insisted that I serve him. "*Mehr Fleisch*," he yelled, attracting general attention. "*Mehr Fleisch, Doktormutter!*"

I could have brained him, but alas, he was too charming. Every imposition was quickly followed by more pleasing flirtation. Upon hearing that my banquet guest, a Mexican girl from my language school, was engaged to her German boyfriend of a year and a half, Max turned to me and asked, "Would you marry me after knowing me for a week and a half?"

3

One thing I can be thankful for, when contemplating my premature midlife crisis, is that I hid my feelings along with my age. This point was confirmed by my Mexican friend, who told me that I looked at Max with a face that said, "Like, *whatever!*" This expression stood me in good stead when Max invited me for a walk in the woods behind the school, apparently for the sole purpose of asking me—once again—my age. ("Well, you *cahn't* be over *thirty!*") The mask must have slipped, though, on the boiling hot day of the college festival, when I spent an hour or two hanging around Max's DJ booth and bringing him food and water.

I was not the only antique in the neighborhood. Hanging around the stage, examining the cables, was a skinny, balding man on the cusp of his forties. Max introduced him to me as his friend and business partner. Kahl had some interest in a Canadian mine; it sounded dodgy to me. We exchanged desultory comments about Bre-X and Canada between ferocious bouts of local German dialect between him and Max. Finally he made some remark about wanting to settle down some day.

"Then you could have some children," I said vaguely.

"Would you like to have children with me?" said Kahl, sleazily.

"Ha ha," I said.

There was a torrent of local dialect between him and Max.

"How many years do you have left to have children?" asked Kahl.

Stunned, I took refuge in exaggeration: "I don't know. Twenty?"

Kahl looked confused. Fuming, I made my escape.

I was furious, and the primary object of my fury was not Kahl but Max. Had Max deliberately encouraged the age-appropriate Kahl to hit on me? I sat in the woods and sulked until the darkly gathering clouds threatened to burst. A wind blew and the air snapped with electricity. As I crossed the college meadow, Kahl approached me.

"There you are!" he said. "Come and have dinner with us. Isn't this storm romantic?"

"*Sturm und Drang*," I said.

Apparently "*Sturm und Drang*" did not mean what I thought it meant, for Kahl smiled wolfishly.

"First the *Sturm*, then the *Drang*," he said smugly.

"I'll just get my purse," I said, and disappeared for the duration of the evening.

"Did Max tell you how to get to his birthday party?" asked my seminarian pal Stefan, phoning a few days later.

"I wasn't invited," I said.

Stammering, Stefan said something about Max's house being very small. I had mercy and told him that I was going out to watch a soccer game.

"That should be really fun!" said Stefan, relieved.

And a few days after that, when I visited him at his rectory, Stefan was full of news.

"I think I know why you weren't invited to Max's party!" he said.

"The house was too small?" I guessed.

"No. It turns out that his friend, that guy who hit on you, was there."

"Ew," I said. "I'm glad I wasn't there, then. Why was *he* there?"

"He's Max's uncle."

After that, I still admired Max's handsome face. I was still struck to the heart when he wore the blue shirt that matched his eyes exactly. But from then on it was a purely aesthetic experience. For the most part, I was cured.

Supporting Seminarians

I know a woman named Emma who sews habits for Dominican novices. She recently asked me, "As the number of young men accepting God's call to the priesthood increases, young women are facing the question of how to interact with these seminarians. How do we appropriately encourage them in their God-given vocation?"

Now, once again, this is a funny question for me, scourge of the seminary, to answer. But never mind me: the important thing is the word "increases." Are things looking up? Let me tell you a story.

In 1814, the Church in Europe was in ruins, thanks to revolutionaries and that villain Napoleon. Vocations had been at rock bottom for some time. The Church looked as if it were down for the count. But then in 1814, the number of vocations began to rise and did not stop rising until 1960. Then they fell with a clunk, but never mind that. The period between 1814 and 1960 was an extraordinarily rich one, with new orders, new sodalities, new ministries, and an explosion of missionary activity. All this after it looked like the Church had taken a knock-out punch.

"Of course, vocations are doomed," said a professor to my class in my American theology school. Well, words along those lines. He looked solemn, but not altogether displeased. One would think this strange, of course, as he was a priest himself. "We are going to have to find new ways to—."

I stuck my hand up after he had finished his grand suggestion.

"Yes, Dorothy?"

"But what about the increase in vocations to more conservative orders?" I asked.

"What about them?" he snapped.

"W-Well, the Tennessee Dominicans, for example, have had to add a building to their convent because so many women are joining. And the Legionnaires of Christ are attracting many men. Of course, the Jesuits are holding their own…."

"I think you should check your facts," sneered the priest,

and went on at great length, growing redder and redder in the face and more and more incoherent. I was shocked and mortified—but that doesn't matter. What matters is that Emma is sewing away for dear life because vocations are on the rise, no matter what neurotic naysayers might splutter. Hooray!

So what to do about all these new seminarians, eh? The world has changed immeasurably, not just since 1814 but since 1960. The rules have changed, but nobody knows what the new ones are. Since so many young women now work in and for the Church, how are we to interact with these idealistic young seminarians?

First of all, listen to your Auntie Dottie when she tells you that seminarians are not all modeled on St. Dominic Savio. They're not all young. They're not all clever. They're not all holy, and by holy I mean the real thing, not just staring at the ground when women walk by or wearing a t -shirt that says "CATHOLIC—Not Just On Sundays." They're not all chaste. They're not all sure they want to be in the seminary. They are not sacred beings. In fact, they are just a bunch of men with varied personalities, varied spiritualities, varied needs and sexuality. What they have in common is that they are Catholic and think they have been called by God to do and be something very special.

I have been in classes with seminarians for five years now, and so I am drawing on my experiences there. My female classmates and I have made wonderful friends who are seminarians or priests. They are our pals, and we like them very much. But there are also seminarians who dislike women, or fear women, or try to give women their phone numbers, or fall in love with women and go into great weepy vocational crises for which they blame the women.

As seminarians ease into the all-male world of the seminary, a world that no longer exists anywhere else in the West, they immediately think about what they lack. And what they lack are women. Women are happily shut out (No Girls Allowed), but they have also been "given up." Never mind if a seminarian is unpleasant, smelly, spotty and dumb. He believes he has given up Woman, and oh, what a heroic trial that is.

So what I am saying is that the way to act around a seminarian friend is as if he were your brother. Don't treat him with kid gloves, as if he were an important and fragile porcelain statue. On the other hand, don't jolt him around emotionally: he's going through a very intense and unusual time. But do not—I cannot stress this enough—do not take any garbage from him. If he dislikes women, avoid him or, if you have to work with him, confront him directly when he is insulting. If he decides to act out on his sexuality and start playing emotional games with you, confront him with that, too. Don't get caught up in a seminarian's psychodrama. *It might not end at his ordination.* "I'd leave but I'm afraid of the rector" has turned into "I'd leave but I'm afraid of my bishop" for other women. It could happen to you. *Don't let it.*

In general, I would advise women to leave their male friends who have gone into the seminary alone for the first year. The guys are finding new friends and new ways in the strange all-male society of the seminary. But afterward they might be wondering what is going on in the rest of the world. If they are smart, they won't eschew female friendship completely, because the priesthood can be a very lonely life, and I firmly believe all men need *some* female companionship. However, they might not deserve it. Like all other men (and women, too), seminarians have to *earn* respect, not assume it is their right, a perk of God's call.

Once I was sitting in a beautiful garden at dusk with a German seminarian. We were talking about vocations.

"I don't really have a vocation," I moaned. "Not married, not single, not religious. I have no idea what my vocation is."

"Maybe your vocation is to support seminarians," laughed my friend. "You cheer us up and so we stay in the seminary!"

Well, he has since left the seminary and is dating a girl he has admired for some time, but I think his insight is valuable. If we are friends of seminarians, then we are called to support them, cheer them up and pray that they discern or are strengthened in their vocation.

The Montreal Massacre

On December 6, 1989, a man named Marc Lépine walked into an engineering classroom at the École Polytechnique in Montreal, Quebec, and ordered all the men to leave. The men, including the professor, left. Lépine then proceeded to shoot the women. He was heard to shout, "You're all a bunch of feminists!"

I don't know if those girls were feminists or not. All I know about them is their names and their interest in engineering. They were bright and had been admitted into engineering school whereas Lépine had not. Lépine certainly didn't canvass them for their political views. Despite his words, I don't think he shot them because they were "feminists." He shot them because they were women. Women who were smarter and more successful than he.

Roman Catholic theology, like engineering, is a predominantly male discipline. Until Vatican II, theology was restricted to seminaries, and thus women, even nuns, could not study it formally. At my old university there was a story about an intrepid nun professor who attended seminary lectures hidden behind a pillar. Like many, if not most, of her generation of women theologians, she is a feminist.

Vatican II happened just before the feminist and sexual revolutions of the 1960s and 1970s. The historical circumstances led to both helpful and bizarre theologies. The excesses of the 1970s still haunt us to this day. If you are a woman studying theology at the graduate level, it is assumed that you are a more-or-less doctrinaire feminist. I find this useful: it makes my traditionalist tendencies less apparent to those who would be frightened by them.

On the other hand, there are those people who, unnerved by the feminist revolution, have a problem with women studying theology at all. Others, convinced that the priesthood is the *sine qua non* of Catholic theology, ask why we bother. Some women, frightened into fits by slanders upon Benedict XVI *et al.* are worried that they will never get ahead professionally if they choose theology as their discipline. All of these objections are nonsense.

On December 6, at my first theology school, I sometimes wondered what would happen if an angry male reject burst into my class with a gun and ordered the men out. Would the Jesuit professor and the scholastics leave us women to die? And here is my belief: No, they would not. They would be terrified, but they would not leave. *Ad majorem Dei gloriam.*

Men We Love

Every once in a while, a woman's magazine will trumpet the headline "Men We Love" and I will flip to the article and see all the high-quality photos of quasi-professional celebrities.

Here in this book, I can't give you splashy photographs

of men I love. And I won't even do a series of pseudonymous profiles because I don't want to embarrass the men I admire. So instead I will just write some things that strike me as admirable in men I have known.

1. **Throwing Things.** Ensconced in an all-girls school, I was thrilled when I made all kinds of male friends in my last year. One of them was sleek and rather boneless. The other boys made fun of him. Although I had a big crush on him, I went along with the idea that he was kind of girly. Well, one day some of the boys played a game of catch. And I saw my crush object throw a baseball. He threw a baseball like it was the most natural thing on earth. In that one movement, he was no longer girly. He was a man transformed.

2. **Approaching Homeless People.** I never know quite what to do when I see a person stretched out under a blanket in the middle of the sidewalk. Is this person sleeping? Is he passed out? Is he dead? Should I talk to him? Should I find a phone and call an ambulance? What would Jesus do? What would Jesus do if he were a tiny woman, somewhat squashy, like me? But the last time I saw such a homeless person, I was with my old pal Stefan, who just went up to the blanket and said in a very thick German accent, "Hello! Are you all right?" It turns out that we were across the street from a shelter, and the homeless guy was napping while waiting for the

shelter to open. I was very proud of Stefan. I was glad he was in clericals.

3. **Rescuing Small Children.** One day when we were at the Canadian National Exhibition, my father suddenly dashed off to the left. He caught a child who had slipped from his seat on the revolving swings and may have been choking on the crossbar. The ride attendant flipped the switch and the ride stopped. I was startled, frightened and very, very proud.

4. **Honor for Marriage.** Once upon a time, I worked for a form of government security and read forms while grilling people. I had an elegant elderly couple before me and the Mrs. had forgotten to fill in the marital status box on her form.

"Of course she's married," said her husband sternly.

She laughed.

"Well, of course," she said kindly, with a little smile, "we could be just living together."

"Tsk!" he said, shocked. "Don't lower yourself!"

His wife laughed. They were totally into each other after all those years. And I just loved that cranky old dude.

5. **Loyalty to Sisters.** One day I was having a phone conversation with my eldest brother. I don't remember if he was calling from work or from military camp or what. Behind him I heard some guy make an unintelligible remark. And my brother, who had been cheerfully

chatting away, made an ice-cold aside: "Hey, that's my *sister*."

6. **More Loyalty to Sisters.** Sometimes my other brother goes out for the evening with my younger sisters. Once we were sitting on the bus when he told me about going to a bar with the older of the two. Some guy, wanting to talk to our pretty blonde sister, bought my brother a drink. My brother took the drink, but his attitude was obvious: "Sucker!" The guy thought he could make my brother lower his guard by buying him a drink. It didn't work. I felt a great rush of affection as I watched my brother smirk over the idea that he could be bribed to turn a blind eye to losers trying to pick up his sisters.

7. **Watching Their Language Before Ladies.** I e-mailed a German friend asking what swear words the Red Baron, about whom I was writing, might have permitted himself to say in front of a lady. Volker wrote back something like *"Any Prussian officer in the First World War would rather have cut out his tongue with a cavalry saber than use obscenities in front of a lady."* The one time I ever heard Volker himself swear, he had just fallen on the ice in front of me and sprained his ankle.

8. **Humility.** I know a great guy who married young. A talented teacher, he now has six children. Anyway, he used to say of his fiancée (now wife), "She thinks I'm a nice guy. I guess I fooled her! Ha ha ha ha ha!"

9. **Toughness.** I once knew a Royal Navy vet. He was torpedoed in the North Sea during World War II *twice*. As an old man, when death approached, he wept a lot. However, he was still pretty tough. When a gang of punks set upon him one time, he sized them up and said in his working-class English accent, "Look here. I was in the Royal Navy. And in the Navy they taught us several ways to kill people. And if you don't bugger off, you'll find out personally." They fled. I suspect the vet shook all the way home.

10. **Tender Hearts.** I had the honor of helping plan that brave man's funeral. He was very against organized religion, so I drew heavily on Royal Navy and Sussex stuff. An old Navy buddy of his, very straight backed, was given the job of reading Tennyson's *Crossing the Bar*. Well, the proper old Navy buddy broke down at the end. And that is something I notice about gruff old soldiers, including my own brother: they are stand-up men, tough, don't give way before other men, but inside the burly chests their hearts are made of soft-serve ice cream. And that is the kind of man I love.

Carbon, Dating

High-Intellectual Romance

When I was in high school, I thought university would be the height of intellectual romance, with professors in tweed, casement windows open against vine-covered walls, and sherry parties in handsome rooms lined with books. My hopes were not completely destroyed: occasionally there are pockets of high-intellectual romance to make up for bad Chablis, windowless classrooms and professors in polyester. Such a pocket is my favorite class this term: Christian Latin.

Christian Latin class takes place in a small departmental library lined with books, sanctified by Eastern Orthodox icons and, above the bookcases, decorated with scenes of ancient ports. There is barely enough room for all seven students and the professor. We sit around a large wooden table in the center, our portly, grey-haired teacher at the head. He wears a tweed jacket, a wool vest and a tie. My only professor here to do so, he begins class with prayer:

"Oremus. Concede mihi, misericors Deus, quae tibi placita sunt …"

Prayer having been said (*ablative absolute*), the Professor says something like, "Now where were we? The *Vexilla*?"

"We're not there yet," someone volunteers. "We still have to do the other *Pange Lingua*."

"Still. Dear, dear. I thought we were farther ahead. All right. Mr. Consalvi. Would you begin, please."

Mr. Consalvi is twenty-one years old, tops. The Professor always but *always* addresses us by title and surname. The only student who doesn't get a title is Mr. Consalvi's nineteen-year-old brother; he is addressed as Consalvi Minor. It was months before I knew my classmates' Christian names. When I bumped into my left-hand neighbor at Benediction one evening, I apologized for not remembering his name. He looked severe and said, "I'm Mr. Liddell." I think he's twenty.

I am the only graduate student, and I feel like a sophomore compared to these old college hands. Consalvi Minor, who really is a sophomore, gives me looks of fellow feeling when our classmates translate rings around us. And around the table we go, Mr. Liddell, Miss Cummings, Mr. Lewis, Miss Short, Mr. Van Buren, Consalvi Minor, Mr. Consalvi and the Professor, who calls out our names at random.

"Mr. Lewis, take us home."

I enjoy the crystal clarity of this class. Graduate theology features a lot of subjective balderdash, but in Christian Latin you are either right or wrong, and the Professor demands a defense of your translation. ("What is the *case*, Mr. Van Buren?") I enjoy also the personalities of my fellow students. Mr. Liddell, tall, dark and handsome, meditates on Tolkien day and night. Mr. Lewis, bearded and bespectacled, is a vociferous Latin Nerd. ("I can't BELIEVE this terrible translation. In *my* parish we use the 1940s hymnal.") Miss Short, tall, tanned and beautifully dressed, is a superb Latinist. Mr. Van Buren, wavy of hair and sleepy of eye, is a quiet, peaceful soul. Mr. Consalvi, handsome and heavy-browed, is restless and intense. His younger brother is meek, mild and astonishingly beautiful, like a Renaissance painting of St. John.

Undergrad Party!

Today I am officially cool.

The Christian Latin class was very giggly this afternoon. It is Friday, after all, and today's Mass preface—and class prayer—asked God to "stir up our hearts." Our hearts were definitely stirred up. We joked and ragged at each other. Consalvi Minor looked at my red T-shirt and asked if I were wearing it for AIDS Awareness Day. The truth is, yes, I am wearing it for AIDS Awareness Day, but in Boston such statements are dangerously divisive, and it is a wise Catholic who discerns whom and how to answer. Consalvi Minor's voice held just enough irony for me to say, "Yes, Consalvi Minor, I am wearing this shirt to remind you not to shoot up heroin until you are married." That settled Consalvi Minor, who smiled sweetly and went back to being meek and mild while the others made fun of him.

After class, I encountered Consalvi Minor, Mr. Consalvi,

Mr. Liddell and Mr. Lewis in the quad. They were talking about a party.

"You made it in," said Mr. Consalvi to me, darkly smirking.

"Made it in where?"

"My party," said Mr. Consalvi. "You made it in."

"I'm being invited to an undergrad party?!"

I could not keep the awe out of my voice. An undergrad party! At my school, undergrad parties are notorious. Notorious!

"Made it in where?" asked Mr. Lewis, having lost the thread.

"Never mind. *You* didn't make it in," said Mr. Consalvi.

"What?"

"Just kidding. The party. You can bring wine," he said to me.

"Okay."

Heck, I'd have agreed to bring a thirty-dollar bottle of vodka if he'd asked. *Undergrad party!*

You must understand. Graduate-student parties in Boston are strained affairs featuring conversations with other people's spouses. I am pathetically grateful to be invited to them, but I wouldn't last an hour without plenty of booze. We tend to have polite, grown-up conversations that will not hurt us politically. The wildest we get is gossiping about which theologians had mistresses:

"Rahner did."

"No, Rahner certainly did not. They were just friends. She was happily married."

"Okay, but Barth did."

"Well, I admit the possibility."

And even when we have drunk too much, we are drawn into philosophical discussions. At one party, I was positively weaving when somebody asked me to explain Lonergan's cognitional theory. Reader, I did. At length. The shame.

Thus I am very much looking forward to this undergrad party. As both Mr. Lewis and Mr. Consalvi are twenty-one, I don't suspect them of inviting me solely because I can buy alcohol legally. It does occur to me, however, that they can't have any idea of just how creakingly old I am. But I don't care: I am cool.

The White Queen

I am back from the undergrad party at the shockingly early hour of 12:36 AM. When I arrived home, I sat wearily at the kitchen table and had another premature midlife crisis. I am not sure what was more exhausting: wandering guiltily around the sophomore dorm with a bottle hidden in my briefcase, or arriving at the party to find a room crammed with pop, chips and super-egos. I don't know what the conservative student newspaper is thundering on about: the assembled undergrads all stared at the brown paper–covered bottle like it was an unexploded bomb.

"I'm not risking getting anybody expelled, am I?" I stammered to the real host, not Mr. Consalvi, the author of my misfortune.

"Well," he said. "*You* can drink it."

I stood by the fridge awkwardly, too afraid to open the bottle. I needed a drink. At a graduate student party, I would already have had a drink. I smiled in that fake-calm way I smile at parties before the drink kicks in. But one thing I could count on: at least no one would ask me to explain a theological point. And there was handsome Mr. Van Buren, coming to rescue me.

"So what did you do today?" he asked.

"I read some Aquinas. I'm writing a paper on Christian response to religious insult."

"What does he say?"

I told him. At length. The shame. He was quite interested, but my own eyes glazed over. Also, I was distracted by the host and another undergrad who were staring at the brown-papered bottle.

"What *is* it?" asked the undergrad in a hushed voice.

The host moved the bottle beside the refrigerator, out of the line of sight of the door to the hallway. We watched *The Lion, the Witch and the Wardrobe* movie. The undergrads made jokes about the relationship between the thirty-something Queen of Narnia and ten-year-old Edmund. Ha ha. A tiny diamond sparkled on Mr. Consalvi's fiancée's ring finger. I think she is twenty. She is certainly beautiful.

Afterwards, they told Catholic jokes that were old when I was seventeen. Mr. Consalvi threw chips at Consalvi Minor's open mouth. Consalvi Minor caught one. We sang "Happy Birthday" to Mr. Lewis. He had turned twenty-two. I realized that I was the only woman there in a low cut top. Consalvi Minor said he liked my boots.

God bless you, please, Mrs. Robinson. I'm going to bed.

Truth Is What Is

I am not at my Seraphic Single best today. One of the draw-backs of trying to live like a twentysomething when you are thirtysomething is that you can't get away with going to bed at two, getting up at eight, and living on coffee and bagels. You get tired and sick. I once heard a woman say that taking care of her children meant that she took care of herself. I believe it. If you're a good mother, checking the food guide and putting balanced meals on the table every day, you are probably eating well, too. I ate very well when friends came to visit. It is harder to take care of just me.

It is hard to live in reality. Life seems too difficult without a few illusions. My favorite illusion is that I am not *really* thirty-five, that I can still pass for twenty-six, and that I will be young forever. However, the bathroom mirror this morning revealed the inescapable truth: be you in school, be you unmarried, be you childless, *be you invited to undergraduate parties*, time will still have its say, and time will still have its way.

The upside of this truth is that you and I are not alone. We are none of us getting any younger, as my grandmother used to say. I was quite fed up with life and singledom and handsome undergraduates by the time Boston Girl and I went to Coffee Hour after Mass today. But then I saw Volker standing there with a cup of coffee.

Unlike Mr. Consalvi, Consalvi Minor, Mr. Liddell and Mr. Van Buren, Volker is no slender young beauty. In fact, he rather looks like Dag Hammerskjöld and is about forty. I imagine he got his doctorate long ago. And when he came up to greet me by the coffee table, I said, in all sincerity,

"How nice to talk to a man my age!"

German in America

I look Irish, so it comes as a surprise to friends to learn that I am part German on my father's side. My American grandmother was a proud *Deutschamericanerin,* and I was not. The burden of that heritage was not one I wanted. I got most of my information about Germans from TV, which does not paint a pretty picture of *Deutschland, oder?* But then I went, terrified, to Germany to learn German, and I fell in love. The clean streets. The tidy neighborhoods. The incomparably efficient public transit system with its musical computer voice. (*"Die nächste Haltestelle ist…Balduinstraße."*) The people who look like my dad when he's concentrating and doesn't want to be disturbed. I loved them. Other foreigners—and younger Germans dying to leave—thought I was crazy. But thanks to my turbulent twenties, I long for quiet, order and people who take fifteen years to open up.

When I returned to Boston I discovered that the city is full of Germans studying away at all the major universities. Some of them even go to church, which is unusual, I assure you. There I met Volker. Volker is quiet. I believe he spends his days in a Cambridge lab, splitting molecules. I practice *The Rules* on him, which at this point usually means not looking at him or talking to him first, and noticing if he looks at and talks to me. And although I am a Seraphic Single, I wondered (out of the pure disinterested desire to know, you understand) if my assiduous practice of *The Rules* would lead him to ask me out.

And lo, in the fullness of time, he sent a group e-mail asking if I (and two others) would go to a concert with him the following night. But alas. As all Rules Girls know, I had to say "No." My female friends applauded, but my male housemates did not. "He's a Science Guy," they said. "He's not going to learn to ask you before Thursdays. He's just going to ask you out on Sunday for Monday." I stewed over this opinion in a most un-Seraphic fashion. And then I did a sneaky thing: I sent a group e-mail to three men, including Volker, asking them how to get to this weekend's German film festival. And Volker replied, with a link giving directions, saying that he might go himself. He did *not* say, "Why don't we go together?" so I assumed he was a lost cause. Such was my reward for breaking *The Rules*.

But then, there I was in a Harvard theater last night when Volker arrived. And, my dears, under our small talk, I was terribly, terribly nervous. When the movie was over, I was hit with a wave of acute discomfort. Do you know that terrible moment when you turn to put on your coat, and you think, "Oh my goodness, now we have to *talk*"? Argh. And in my case, I didn't know what the situation was. Was it a date? A half date? A mere bumping into each other accidentally? Or accidentally on purpose? I like clarity, and clarity I did not have. He helped me with my coat. What did that mean? And he saw me to my cab in Harvard Square, and didn't leave until I was inside. What did that mean? Anything? Nothing?

All in all, my sister Singles, I think I will in future resist any temptation to break *The Rules*, even a little bit.

The Go-Between

When Boston Girl had laryngitis, I brought her some chicken soup and my copy of *The Rules*. Boston Girl drank the soup, listened to *The Rules* and was instantly converted to the Gospel of Ellen Fein. No longer would she approach men first, show too much interest or ask them out. She would join the disciplined ranks of the Rules Girls. Also, she would go to my parish church, which, unlike her parish church, is a gold mine of well-educated Catholic bachelors our age and older. And that is how she came to meet Czech Boy.

Czech Boy is tall, slender, blond, bespectacled and, well, Czech. He is very handsome and has a dry sense of humor. *I* met him *first*, but he didn't try to impress *me*. Indeed, he told me that he, like all Czechs, is miserable and pessimistic and that he is the worst of them all. All righty, then. But when I introduced Boston Girl to Czech Boy, and she cleverly ignored him to talk to his friend about her Slovak roots, Czech Boy was all smiles. When Boston Girl, heart beating like a drum, deigned to talk to Czech Boy, they fell deeply into a conversation about Dvorak and other Czechoslovak topics. He did not ask for her number, but Boston Girl and I felt that the foundation had been set.

The next week, Boston Girl and I took our post-Mass coffee over to the seating area where Czech Boy was talking to the Doyen of Coffee Hour. We nodded, but Czech Boy did not come over. So, because Boston Girl couldn't—according to *The Rules*—go over to him, I did. And, also against *The Rules*, I flirted up a storm.

"How is your work going?" I asked brightly.

"Very bad. I wrote only two articles on my blog."

"Really? I wrote seven on mine. But what is your blog about?"

"I am trying to popularize some scientific questions."

"Oh. Well, mine is more general. It is for women."

"I see. I suppose you write about *love*."

"No," I lied. "I can't write about love, for there is no love in my life."

"That is very sad," said Czech Boy, and dropped his voice sexily. "Would you like some love in your life?"

I blinked.

"Just kidding," said Czech Boy more hastily than decency dictated.

"What about you?" I asked. "Is there love in *your* life?"

Czech Boy looked depressed again.

"There was—but no longer."

This boded well for Boston Girl, so I called her over on some pretext. Unfortunately, the Doyen of Coffee Hour then announced that he was carting off Czech Boy for lunch. But Czech Boy tarried, talking for as long as possible to Boston Girl. He asked us to come along for lunch, but of course we couldn't (*The Rules*) and so that was that. Czech Boy asked Boston Girl if she'd be back the next week, which we interpreted as a good omen for the future. But once again he didn't ask for her phone number.

Yesterday, Boston Girl and I went to Mass and afterward to Coffee Hour. At that point I was heavily invested in Boston Girl's happiness and broke *The Rules* left and right on her behalf. I marched up to Czech Boy and his buddy, chatted up a storm (*How did your work go this week? Very bad.*), and said, "Now, where is Boston Girl? I've lost her. Do *you* see her?" This gave me the chance to call her over.

When we were separated from Czech Boy and Co., I got them back by pretending that they had rejected me, and that although I had never wanted to talk to them ever again,

I forgave them. And I managed to unglue a woman from Boston Girl by introducing her to a cute German lawyer, which left Boston Girl free to talk to Czech Boy. Finally, when Czech Boy and Co. said that they had to go to lunch with the missing Doyen, I insisted that we go with them, to give the Doyen a piece of my mind.

Whew. After all that Rule-breaking, I was wiped. But it was worth it because it gave Boston Girl at least another half hour with Czech Boy, and he told her several times that he had come to Coffee Hour to see her. At last, I announced that we had to go shopping and carried Boston Girl away. To our dismay, he had still not asked for her phone number.

"Darn it," I cried. "What more can I do?"

Backsliders

I confess to Ms. Ellen Fein and to you, my Seraphic Singles, that I have broken *The Rules* through my own fault, both in making it incredibly easy for a man to ask me out and in accepting a date for Wednesday on Monday. And I ask all my readers, Seraphic or Searching, and you, my editors and marketers, not to call me names or to stop reading this book.

Okay, that's done. Here's the skinny:

Things have not been going smoothly at Coffee Hour. Czech Boy has not turned up in two weeks. Is he skipping Mass, too? I fear for his soul. Boston Girl has been bearing his absence like a true Bostonian, i.e. saying, "Dude, you're not allowed to feel sorry for me. I hate that." On the other hand, the absent Volker has been turning up again. So it once again fell to me to ignore a man, sit on the couch with my coffee, and wait for him to come over and talk to me first. And he did. We had a merry little conversation. Volker, it turns out, has a vivid and clever sense of humor. Finally, Boston Girl said she had to go home, and I too said I had to go home, and Volker likewise declared such an exigence. Off he went, black overcoat flapping. It was all very sudden. And slightly confusing. Boston Girl and I alighted from the parish center deep in thought.

"When is Volker going to ask me out?" I asked.

"Dude," said Boston Girl. "I've been thinking about that. *The Rules* suck. *The Rules* are never going to work on Volker. He obviously likes you. He just needs more encouragement."

"Darn it," I said. "What more can I do?"

"You're just going to have to break *The Rules*."

"Darn it, I don't want to break *The Rules*. Darn Science Guys. Argh!"

I went home and consulted my ex–Science Guy housemate, Jon. He stood in the kitchen wreathed in cigar smoke and pontificated: "Lookit. Science Guys—they're clueless. And Science *Gals*—well, they're very practical. They're Science Gals. They know what they want. They're very aggressive. My buddy, there was this gal, she actually went to his door to take him out. She was at *his door*. He said, *Okay, just a minute*, and he climbed out his bedroom window."

Well, compared to that, I was an Aloof Unavailable Ice Queen no matter what. After some hours, I sent an e-mail. It expressed a question, the fruit of the pure, disinterested desire to know: "*Dear Volker, Why on earth do you not ask me out for coffee? Dorothy.*" And the next morning, instead of receiving the answer to this mystery, I got an invitation: "*Dear Dorothy, I just had a great idea. Why don't we meet for coffee? What about Wednesday? Volker.*"

"Give me Czech Boy's e-mail," said Boston Girl.

Babel

M y first boyfriend threatened to kill me. Weary and dispirited after weeks of fending off his advances, I took his threat for what it was: Middle Eastern hyperbole. Given our rather innocent and ordinary teenage relationship, the statement "If I find you with another man, I will kill you" was as silly and mawkish as one of his beloved Persian pop songs. "Go ahead," I said. "It would make me a legend at school." Aziz thought my answer was hilarious and squashed me in a great bear hug.

Aziz was a fairly recent immigrant plucked by his more-established brother from the Red Cross camp in which he had been languishing. The ruins of their middle-class existence were housed in a beat-up rental on a dodgy downtown street. They occupied three rooms: a front parlor, an adjoining bedroom and a kitchen. Aziz slept in the kitchen. The front parlor had a magnificent Persian carpet, a mysterious hanging bronze lamp or kettle, and a Quran on the highest shelf. The apartment smelled of oily spicy food and of Aziz's brother's Italian cologne. Thanks to Aziz, my first encounter with Islam was more Arabian Nights than Al-Qaeda. And the Quran, which said Aziz wasn't allowed to have sex before marriage, was my friend.

I ditched Aziz when the confusion got too onerous. It was not just the pressure to put out (which, in retrospect, was comparatively mild), it was his lack of English. He pretended not to understand English when it was convenient, but at other times he pretended to understand more English than he did. I decided that from then on, I would date only men who were fluent in English. And for the most part I have, with the possible exception of Jean-Pierre, who hadn't got the hang of metaphors yet. ("*Tabernoosh!* It's raining kittens and puppies!") It is hard enough to communicate with men without ESL problems getting in the way.

I am thinking about this because of Volker. For some reason, Volker, who is a very nice man in person, seems to turn into a scarred veteran of the Battle Between the Sexes in print. In his last e-mail, he insisted that he respects the only female member of his research team: *Yesterday she brought us brownies.* If these are jokes, they are a little heavy-handed. I am hoping it is a language thing.

Nice Catholic Boys

The tale may now be told. Boston Girl has given me permission to tell you of Czech Boy, whom we now call Atheist Boy. (Guess why.) Boston Girl and I are not so much religious conservatives as we are ghetto Catholics who, since there are no longer any Catholic ghettos west of Belfast to be a part of, built the ghetto in our own heads. From the outside, we look like ordinary modern Catholic intellectuals, talking knowledgeably about feminist critique and Confucian-Catholic dialogue. But on the inside we are plotting our next attempt to meet Nice Catholic Boys.

It never occurred to Boston Girl and me that there might be atheists lurking by the coffee urn after Mass. For us, Coffee Hour was the last safe hunting grounds of Nice Catholic Girls Over Thirty. And thus, we were out of our minds with rage when we discovered that Czech Boy was neither Nice nor Catholic. In fact, the reason Czech Boy had not asked Boston Girl out, despite his obvious attentions at Coffee Hour, is that he is not interested in relationships. He says he has no time for relationships. Instead, he requires strings-free "animalistic sex" and had thought, correctly, that Boston Girl, being a churchgoing Catholic and all, would not be into that. But he also thought, incorrectly, that perhaps he could change her mind. His sole motive in coming to our church was to meet the well-connected Doyen of the Coffee Hour. Worship of God, in whom Czech/Atheist Boy does not believe, and meeting Nice Catholic Girls, for whom he has no use, did not enter into his considerations. His grandparents fought *for* the Communists. That just seems wrong.

My friend Kelly argues that we are missing the point of Catholic coffee hours, which she envisions as all-welcoming and inclusive of all peoples, not just Catholics. I agree with this in principle, but it does not solve the problem that now there is no foolproof place in which to meet Nice Catholic Boys Over Thirty. I thought I was sharing my gold mine with Boston Girl, and—alas—it has turned up fool's gold.

Who Pays on a Date?

One of the side effects of being single is that sometimes you go on dates. This is one of the obvious things that differentiates real singles from priests, monks and nuns, who do not go on dates. Well, some do, but they don't tell all their friends about it. There are certainly Catholic seminarians who date. I could tell you stories, and I probably will.

Dating, of course, is a drag. It is especially a drag for me because the kindest, most pious, most amusing and best-looking men I know are walled alive in seminaries and monasteries across North America and Europe. And the ones I like are never the bad ones who date. On my most recent trip to Europe, a female friend and I toddled after a most dashing seminarian in the cobblestoned bar district of a large German city. We assured him that on his ordination day, we would cry. "*Doch*," he said, "Nobody will cry for me." Frankly, I had cried *already*, but it wasn't good form to say so. And meanwhile, I had a date on Friday night back in the USA, with dear old Volker, who is not a seminarian. His seminary dream died when he discovered that priests work all week, not just on Sundays.

I don't pay on dates. This is to say, I don't pay for dinner. And I don't pay for drinks. There are two reasons for this. First, I am trying, in my small way, to recreate order. The dating world before us is in pieces, and it is up to women of goodwill to put it back together again. One way to do this is to stubbornly not pay our way when we are on a date, and to stubbornly pay our way when we are not on a date. This underscores what we are doing as we scarf dinner and indulge in high-minded chat. We are either on a Date or we are merely eating together as Friends. Secondly, I've already put down some serious coin on the pre-date. If I paid for the pre-date and then half the date, I would be paying more than the guy who asked me out, and that is just wrong. The pre-date requires, at very least, a manicure. A manicure costs more than some entrees. You do the math. A new lipstick costs between five and ten dollars. A new dress—, well, let's just say that if I buy a new dress, I should have no guilt whatsoever about Mr. Date dropping $100 on dinner to impress me.

The problem is, I do feel guilty when Mr. Date drops $100 on dinner to impress me. And right now I am too utterly broke to pay for anything more than a manicure. So I was glad to discover, by consulting Boston Girl and my housemates, that Volker was not taking me to that kind of restaurant. (My housemate Jon, however, was not impressed. "If he wants to do Italian, he should take you somewhere in the North End," he harrumphed. "Y'know, he could be cheap. Well, he's a Science Guy.") But expense or lack thereof is not the point. The point is that, for some mysterious reason, Volker wanted the pleasure of my company, as my mother would say. How much pleasure was to be had in my company, given that I had wicked jet lag, Volker alone knows. To quote the great Canadian philosopher Bernard Lonergan, objectivity is the fruit of authentic subjectivity. And because Volker did me the honor of asking me to dinner, I did him the honor of getting my nails done.

"Men don't notice nails," said Jon. "Well, it's your money."

Impressed Much

My buddy McKelvie once told me, in a fit of sudden rage, that Shania Twain's "That Don't Impress Me Much" should be my theme song. He ranted and raved a bit. I forget what my crime was; I think it was that I refused to flirt with some philosophy professor he and Ted admired. But it may be because I insisted that, despite what men think, women are not impressed by snazzy cars.

Since then, my ever-helpful housemate Jon has told

me many personal anecdotes about women who try to get a look at his watch, his shoes, and his coat label, and I am reluctantly convinced that maybe men aren't just projecting. Perhaps some women do care about what kind of car men drive. However, I maintain that these women might like guys with snazzy cars because snazzy cars make men happy and confident, and women like happy, confident men.

That said, I have just discovered what impresses me: access to exclusive libraries. Today I got taken on a date to the Widener Library. The Widener Library would normally be closed to me. The Widener Library is for Harvard people alone. I have gotten into a dance club on the strength of my charm, but charm doesn't work on the Widener. But with a flash of his Harvard ID, Volker got me into the Widener Library. And then the Law Library. And then a laboratory, which has all kinds of interesting and doubtlessly expensive Star Trek–like things. And I am impressed. Deeply, soulfully impressed.

My impressions are somewhat foggy, for I kept thinking that any minute I would be thrown out. What if one of the princes or princesses of Harvard took a good look at my proletarian snow boots and called a guard? But perhaps I was taken for a grad student. Or an eccentric professor. Or someone attached to one.

I do recall that the Widener is large, with high ceilings and blue armchairs here and straight-backed chairs there. It was very quiet, and there weren't many students. The wooden tables gleamed softly. There was just the very subtlest smell of wet wool in the hallways. It looked like a very nice place to work. The top floor of the Harvard Law Library made my heart race. It is built on neo-Classical lines, with white walls, a cathedral ceiling and columns. Under the ceiling ran golden mottoes, mostly in Latin, about the Law. The most prominent one was "*Scire Leges Non Hoc Est Verba Earum Tenere Sed Vim Ac Potestatem.*" Flexing my translating muscles, I can tell you that this means "To know the laws is not to grasp just their words but also their force and power." Oooh! Force. *Power.*

It was staggering. I am not usually affected by architecture to that extent. It was almost a relief to go outside and be shown the much homier laboratory where Volker spends his days. For fun he showed me a microscope that is probably worth more than everything I own, and stuck one of my hairs on a slide.

"Let's see what we can find out about Dorothy," he said.

What we found out is that I have split ends. Let that be a lesson to us all to go to the hairdresser regularly. You never know when your hair might end up under a high-powered microscope. Meanwhile, I must say that was the most impressive date venue of my life. I have no idea what kind of car my escort drives. I suspect he depends on public transportation.

The Third-Date Rule Rejected

Before he left Europe, Volker was warned about American dating culture. There is no dating, as North Americans understand it, in Germany. No one explained dating to him, and he thought he would just muddle along and plead cultural ignorance if he got into trouble.

On Thursday, I stared at my computer in consternation. Volker had asked me out not for Friday night, not for Saturday night, but for *Sunday afternoon*. What could it mean? I sought out my housemate Jon to inquire.

"He's avoiding the Third-Date Rule," he said immediately.

"They don't have the Third-Date Rule in Germany. And we've already been on our third date."

"That wasn't a *date*. He doesn't count that as a *date*. *I* wouldn't have counted that as a date. This is definitely about the Third-Date Rule. He's afraid that he's going to get too physical and stuff, and that is why he picked Sunday afternoon."

"But we're Catholic. We have nothing to do with the Third-Date Rule."

"Or maybe," said Jon, "it's just his way of showing that he doesn't like you that much."

Oh, *please*.

The Third-Date Rule is a popular North American convention that states that if two people do not have sex on the third date, the relationship is doomed and a waste of time. It is also evidence that Satan makes up his own commandments in mockery of our loving God. I only became aware of the Third-Date Rule two years ago, but my housemate says it has been around since the 1970s.

"Hey," he said, "It's an improvement on the 1960s."

I learned of the Third-Date Rule in the most unpleasant way possible short of rape. Having taken me on the Coffee Date and the Dinner Date, my suitor invited me for a meal at his mother's apartment. Charmed, I bought flowers for the mother. However, although the pink and frilly apartment was obviously a mother's, there was no mother to be seen. My suitor made risotto, played romantic music and invited me to slow dance after dinner. It was obviously a cheap seduction scene.

"Where is your mother?" I finally asked.

"What?" He laughed. "Did you think I had her hidden somewhere?"

She had gone to spend that night at her boyfriend's place, leaving her apartment free for "us." She was sixty-eight. Society has gone to hell in a handbasket, people.

The best way to avoid the unpleasant Third-Date Rule situation, I think, is to allude to its stupidity before the Third Date. Another way, of course, is to tell all suitors or beloveds on the *First* Date that you are a traditional Christian, Jew, Muslim, Hindu, Buddhist, etc. at heart. The downside of this approach is that you will not get a Second Date quite a lot of the time. You might not have the lighthearted and flirtatious period leading up to the Third Date. However, these are perilous times, times in which the Third-Date Rule can flourish despite the cardinal rule of "No Means No," and you must be strong. Your reward is that you winnow out all the losers who either just want to get laid or are caught in the trap of serial monogamy.

I brought up the Third Date-Rule to Volker last week, writing that European women would probably find it a nasty surprise. And Volker wrote back, "European women would be outraged by the very idea that they could be obliged to do anything for no matter how many dinners." So let us all do as sophisticated European women do, and give the Third-Date Rule the scorn it so richly deserves.

The Surprise Fourth-Date Surprise

Boston Girl and I stepped out of the American Gothic building into the frozen Cambridge afternoon.

"Dude," said Boston Girl. "I thought your head was going to explode."

"I know it is Harvard," I raged, "but it's Harvard-freakin' *Div!* Okay, like, I am actually from a respectable theology department. They should be glad I want to take their freakin' course. I don't know why I have to jump through freakin' hoops to get into a class at Harvard Div. I wouldn't bother except one of my profs back home told me to take a class here so as to hear the conversations in the hallways. I mean, it's the freakin' heart of loony-tunes, whacked out, bizarre, heretical, post-Christian—"

"Dude," said Boston Girl. "Chill."

"And I still can't believe Volker asked me out for Sunday afternoon. What about Friday? This is Friday. What's he doing?"

"Maybe he can't afford to take you out for dinner."

"I've thought of that," I said, calming down. "His corporate sponsors are in jail."

"Well, there you go. I'm starving."

We went to Harvard Square and ate burritos. Boston Girl ate with gusto, rolling her eyes. I chewed soberly, meditating on Friday nights versus Sunday afternoons. Eventually, Boston Girl finished eating and resumed her workaholic ways.

"Dude, I gotta go read."

"Me, too. See you later."

But I didn't go directly to my usual café. First I went into a library to see if Volker had e-mailed. Still innocent of American dating rules, Volker had never asked for my phone number. And I, obedient to *The Rules*, had never called him. And I was glad to discover that he had e-mailed because he explained why he had asked me out for Sunday, which was simply that I would be in Cambridge anyway. He had absolutely no idea that a Sunday-afternoon invitation (as opposed to Friday or Saturday night) could be construed as lack of interest. He seemed distressed.

Poor Volker, I thought. In his field, he does not have to think about the vagaries of human behavior. There is no guesswork; only hypotheses. There are no unwritten rules, or rules cobbled together in a moral vacuum, or even *The Rules.* There is no brooding about Friday versus Sunday. In the natural world, things just fall into place. Perhaps I should behave as if I lived on the molecular level. Perhaps I should just fall into place, accepting things as they come. And maybe I should stop following *The Rules.*

I wrote these philosophical reflections to Volker and mentioned where I would be if he'd like to drop by. Feeling cheerful, I went to my café and read neo-Platonic sermons for three hours. At about six, in a laboratory some blocks away, Volker misread my deep thoughts and panicked. He grabbed his coat.

"Would you like to go for a walk," he said, appearing at my table.

It was not a question.

I looked out at the black and freezing street and most definitely did not want to go for a walk. I wanted to stay in my nice warm café and read neo-Platonic sermons. Not only was it cold out there, I could sense Strong Emotion in the air. And if there is anything that frightens members of my family, it is Strong Emotion. Not impatience or irritation, obviously, but the heavy stuff. My mother expresses affection by lightly hitting us with paper-towel tubes.

Intellect—we are all about intellect. If Volker had looked

like he was going to lecture me on nuclear physics, I would have felt fine. But he looked like he was going to make a Speech, one inspired by Strong Emotion. He held my coat. Helpless before such chivalry, I obediently slipped my arms in. Doomed! Doomed! We stepped into the frozen Cambridge night.

Volker made his Speech. I wish I could tell you exactly what he said, but I was barely listening. I was too traumatized by the presence of Strong Emotion. I would remind myself to listen and that this was important, but then I would tune out again in panic. For two minutes, I thought he was condemning American dating conventions. For another two minutes, I thought he was breaking up with me. And then after another two minutes, I concluded that he was saying that he was willing to go through bizarre American dating practices for my sake. His English, usually perfect, was decidedly wonky.

"And that's what I wanted to say," said Volker.

I let out the breath I had been holding for six minutes.

"Well, I'm totally traumatized," I said. "Let's go have a beer."

"Good idea," said Volker. "But let's walk through Harvard Yard first."

We walked through Harvard Yard and stopped to look at the trees. They were black against the shadowy buildings. It was very, very cold.

"Harvard Yard is very beautiful at night," said Volker.

"Yes, it is," I said.

And then he kissed me.

Canadian Dating

Canada is a nation of contrasts. It has a monarchy, and yet it is a democracy. It is a wealthy capitalist country, and yet it is strongly socialist. It has three histories: that of the French-speaking population, that of the English-speaking population, and that of the Aboriginal peoples. Almost half its citizens identify as Roman Catholics on the census, but Canada is no longer a particularly religious country.

Geographically, Canada is the second-largest country in the world, but it has a population of only thirty million. It was arguably the most loyal and productive part of the British Empire, but now the cities swell with a post-WW II multicultural immigrant population so diverse that it is difficult to say just what "a Canadian" is anymore. Traditionally, we have identified ourselves with our relationship to the Canadian wilderness, our increasing independence from Britain and our wary friendship with the United States of America. More recently, our literature also reflects the immigrant experience.

So, too, are our dating practices a study in contrasts. For the most part, the young do not date. They "hook up," which seems to mean that their "romantic" or (at least) sexual relationships begin with a mutual attraction upon which they act as soon as possible. For the most part, male and female high school and college students study together, and they go out in packs until they cut each other temporarily out of the herd, so to speak. I will divide the young into two groups: those whose parents care about female chastity, and those whose parents do not care about female chastity. The former group do not usually engage in sexual relations. The latter group usually do, starting at age thirteen or fourteen. Teen sex is discouraged in the Catholic, Evangelical Christian, Jewish and Islamic schools and places of worship, but apparently is actively encouraged everywhere else.

Once Canadians have left the comfortable, communal villages of high school and college, we no longer have quite so many opportunities to hang around with members of the opposite sex. Therefore, dating happens. Typically, either men or women meet someone we find interesting at work or through friends, and we ask each other for our phone numbers. This may or may not lead to a date, usually for coffee or a drink. Sex on the first date is not unusual, although the marginally more serious-minded wait until the infamous Third Date. If the couple like each other enough, dating is replaced by the old "hanging out" of high school, involving a lot of after-work TV watching and culminating in moving in together. This is seen as a major step in the relationship, one which one or the other half of the couple may resist for a long time. We who marry—often as a reward for years of good sexual and TV-watching service—do so in a ceremony as elaborate and tasteless as we can afford. (Lest I seem unbearably cynical, let me add that I believe that cohabiting couples do sometimes fall sincerely in love.)

Opposed to this approach, a growing minority of people in Canada do not see dating as a way to get sex and company while watching TV. Religious people in particular put a very high value on marriage, and so they see dating as a way to meet and get to know potential spouses. How strictly these dates are supervised (if at all) depends on the ethnic background or religious sensibilities of the parents of the dating couple. Sexual activity is more likely to be delayed, although parish priests usually assume that engaged Catholics are sleeping together.

Many traditional-minded Canadian Catholics ponder the pre–Vatican II question "How far can you go?" while others do a little theological finessing to rationalize what we are up to. This is hardly surprising, as the average Canadian doesn't marry until our late twenties. But, in general, I would guess that churchgoing, unmarried Catholics in Canada follow the teachings about sexual relations better than our co-religionists in the United States. At any rate, we don't make our infractions quite so obvious or talk about them quite so openly or argue quite so confidently that they are not really sins but prophetic actions ushering in the Kingdom of God.

Retro Chic/k

The most frequent profession of feminism I hear centers on the practice of going Dutch on dates. A Boston weekly asked women if they believed in going Dutch; the ones who did said things like, "It's only fair" and "I want to show that I am an equal partner in this relationship." As a poor student, the daughter of a housewife and perhaps even a feminist, I dislike the idea that I am not an "equal partner" in a relationship if I am not coughing up half the financial resources. When did romance become Marxist? I am not exactly sure what makes one an "equal partner," but I doubt it is money.

I brood on this today because I have reached new heights of retro formality and glamour: dinner for two at the Harvard Faculty Club. As I looked nervously around the dining room of this exclusive edifice, I imagined that many writers would give their eyeteeth to see it. It could serve as great backdrop for so many fictional scenes: a scholarly seduction, the treason of a weapons researcher, the murder of an unpopular professor. It would be embarrassing for one's victim to fall dead upon the "midnight blue" carpet when anyone in this university's faculty could tell you that the carpet is, in fact, a rich dark red with a pattern of gold marks.

Above all else, I must say that I deeply enjoyed dinner. It was delicious. Although this may not be true in fact, it appeared to me to be the best of English food cooked by a clever Frenchman. Any British admiral of the past four hundred years would have commended it highly. My host was, as always, very good company. And the Faculty Club was beautiful. It was very much in keeping with the glamour and the glory of Harvard. But I must say that all the formality frightened me a little.

Volker had to show his ID card; that rattled me. The young tuxedoed waiter who asked for it inadvertently intimidated me. The rich, dark red draperies that could be drawn to separate our part of the room from others (if we were Edward VII and Sarah Bernhardt, for example) awed me. And I was struck dumb by the china, which was heavily encrusted with gold. Although the dark world outside was blanketed in snow, expensive-looking blossoms floated in water behind the beautiful salt and pepper shakers. The table, like all the other tables, was richly clothed in starched white linen. It twinkled with silver and crystal. I was grateful that I was covered in jewelry and black velvet; I matched.

"Would you like menus?" asked a second tuxedoed waiter.

"Thank you, I have already ordered," said Volker. "I hope," he said to me in a slightly apologetic tone, "that is all right with you."

"Of course," I murmured, the child of neo-Edwardians.

Apparently, there were once restaurants where ladies were given menus without prices. This was discovered to be an outrageous crime against womyn, so these restaurants might not exist anymore. I rather like that custom; ordering today is always embarrassing because I know how much my host has to shell out to feed me when ramen noodles, consumed at home, would have cost only a dollar a packet. I contemplated the pale gold walls and the rich velvet draperies and suppressed a frugal Ontario shudder. Ordering ahead was *quite* all right with me.

"Would you like the wine list, sir?"

"Thank you," said Volker. "Do you trust me," he enquired of his drapery-contemplating guest, "to choose a good wine?"

"I trust you implicitly," I murmured again. Somewhere Gloria Steinem had a seizure.

My host chose a good wine. Meanwhile, the first and younger waiter had come by to murmur concernedly in my host's ear. How would we like our beef?

"Medium rare," I said. Gloria Steinem recovered. But I was strangely lacking in conversation. Having been relieved of most choices, I wasn't sure what my role was. Without the menu to comment on, what was there to say? And if I could think of it, could I say it in front of the waiter? Hmm…What would Queen Alexandra have done?

When the wine arrived, the waiter indicated the label to Volker, who looked at it with equanimity. After pulling out the cork, the waiter scrunched behind my host's chair to pour him a sample. Volker approved the sample. The waiter scrunched around again to pour me a glass and then had to scrunch back to fill up Volker's glass. It was all very correct and complicated.

For some reason, I began to talk about feminist philosophy. This, naturally, was a blank book to my host, so I switched to Marie Curie, and that was better. Meanwhile, the dinner was continuing along in a positively ritualistic fashion. Dishes were served perfectly. Dishes were removed perfectly. It was all according to the Formal Dining section of my mother's fifty-year-old etiquette book. It was very nice, but it made me feel very, very guilty. It was as if the 1970s had never happened and Women's Studies departments hadn't been thought of yet. What do they do, I wonder, when Judith Butler drops in for a nosh?

And it occurs to me that highly trained waiters aren't stupid. They are taught to be very observant. From the minute my host had taken charge, they had realized which script to follow: the old one.

Ladies and Gentlemen

On Friday I awoke from my nap in the library to discover a howling white wilderness outside the window. The forecast had said "flurries"; I had worn shoes. So instead of walking home, which had become physically impossible, I took a bus and a couple of trains to Cambridge to wait out the storm with Volker.

The twenty-minutes-late bus was packed with students. One of the sitting undergraduate men gave me a nervous smile, which I returned. It had been the kind of day when college people had asked me "Faculty or staff?" so the smile was soothing to my ego. Then the guy next to him got up and offered me his seat.

"Oh no, that's okay. Thank you."

"Take it. I'm getting off soon."

"Well, okay. Thank you. Thank you very much."

After all, I was the only woman within three feet, so I took the seat and beamed at the world. And then the nervously smiling undergrad turned to me.

"Hi," he said.

"Hi," I said.

"I'm sorry I didn't give you my seat before," he said.

"That's okay," I said. "I got one anyway."

"No, you see…Can I tell you the story of why I didn't?"

I was intrigued, and I love stories. Men have given me seats, men have not given me seats, but none have explained their motivations.

"Go right ahead!"

The tale might be a familiar one to you gents. Last week, my neighbor had been in similar circumstances. Crowded bus. Seat scored. Lady hanging off a strap nearby. My neighbor's childhood training kicked in and he offered the woman his seat. And her response was along the lines of: "How dare you! How dare you offer me your seat? Do I look weak? Do I look like I need to sit down? Do I look like I need your seat? You are continuing the evil patriarchal fascism of our times. You should be ashamed of yourself. The patriarchy…(etc.)."

"I was so embarrassed," concluded my neighbor. "There were people all around and everything."

"Well," I said. "I'm sorry that happened to you. How old was this woman? Middle-aged?"

"No, she was a student. I've seen her at school."

My mind boggled at the idea of a college girl in 2007 acting like a helmet-haired working mom of 1984 or a fist-waving protester of 1975.

"But that's so out of date. That girl was an idiot. And rude."

"If my grandparents had seen me not offering you my seat, they would have …" My neighbor's voice trailed off. Then he introduced himself. He was a freshman—probably seventeen or eighteen years old.

There are men who loathe women. There are men who oppress women. There are men who are so worried about women acting up that they exert as much control over them as they can: they make up ridiculous laws about women's appearance and travel and tell them God said so. But I'll tell you something for free: a man never gave up his seat to a woman to oppress her. I've gone out with a control freak who pouted and steamed when I forgot that I wasn't ever allowed to open the door for myself, but I've never felt threatened by a man giving up his seat.

Volker has delightful manners. He holds my coat when I want to put it on. He opens doors. He walks always on the right because in Germany well-brought up men always walk on the right of a lady. And in fact, Volker always makes me feel like a lady, which is nice, because I was brought up to *be* a lady. Being a lady has nothing to do with weakness and everything to do with good manners and moral strength. And from this I am certain that Volker's mother is a lady, for it is she who trained Volker in his good manners. Ladies expect and demand respect from men, and then they instill respect for women in their own sons. And they never, never, ever scream at a stranger in public for old-fashioned signs of respect. If my neighbor had grabbed her butt, the privileged, private college attending Feminist Avenger would have had a case. As it is, I think she was just a mean-spirited wretch.

The Kind You Get a Crush On

Like many other girlfriends, I want to know who the competition is, especially when it is sparse, foreign and fifteen years out of date.

"So who did you have a crush on in high school?" I asked Volker.

Volker thought long and hard. Possibly some man in some lab in some country had warned him never to answer a question like this.

"Well, I thought Tanya was very attractive," he said at last.

Bleak irony of fate! I have met Tanya. She is very attractive indeed, alas.

"You had a crush on Tanya!?"

"No, I said I was *attracted* to Tanya. I didn't have a crush on her."

"You were attracted to her, but you didn't have a crush on her?"

And then Volker uttered a truth so sharp, so startling, so...so *true*, that if we could get a hundred pages out of it, we would have ourselves a best-selling book: *"There is the kind of girl you are just attracted to, and the kind you get a crush on."*

When I think of the time I've wasted trying to be more attractive, I could eat another bowl of Ben and Jerry's ice cream. (*Excuse me a second...Back now. Mmmm!*) As a child I thought designer jeans were the answer. As a teen I thought miniskirts and big flashy earrings were the answer. As a twentysomething adult I thought looking like G.I. Jane was the answer. And all my life I have had long conversations with friends searching for the answer. *What do men want?* we wondered. *Good God, what do men want?*

"Joke about your underwear," said my friend Gina one day six years ago.

Gina was a tiny blonde ex-cheerleader. Men threw themselves at her feet. She smashed hearts left and right until she herself fell for a German intellectual.

"I can't joke about my *underwear!*" I said, outraged.

"Sure you can. It always, always, *always* works. If you joke about your underwear, a guy will think about you in your underwear, and then he will ask you out."

"I work in an office as a temp," I said. "There are no opportunities to joke about underwear."

"Make one," said Gina. "Trust me."

My office was not the kind of place where a temp could make underwear jokes. However, I kept what Gina said in mind. Valentine's Day rolled around, and my boring oppressors floated around the office sporting red accessories. Somehow I had missed the dress code memo. The silver-haired cutie from down the hall eyed me in the photocopy room.

"It's Valentine's Day," he said flirtatiously. "Why aren't you wearing any red?"

Gina's directive popped into my mind.

"How do YOU know I'm not wearing any red?" I asked.

The silver-haired cutie turned crimson.

"Why did you SAY that? Now how am I supposed to work?"

"And we dated for two years after that," I told Volker.

Volker had a good laugh. But then he frowned. Possibly Volker does not enjoy hearing about the competition, no matter how sparse, foreign and out of date. But instead of sulking, he looked very strict indeed, perhaps as strict as his aristocratic ancestor Volker von Zwei.

"Respectable Catholic girls do not wear red underwear," he growled.

Although I laughed until I cried, I realized it was that kind of statement that makes Volker the kind I get a crush on.

Devil in a Green Shirt

It was St. Patrick's Day. The phone rang. It was Boston Girl.

"Dude! You gotta come out. I'm so drunk. There's a guy at the bar who keeps buying me drinks. I'm going to make out with him."

"Where are you?"

"I'm in—Where are we? We're in James's Gate. In Jamaica Plain. Dude, I am so going to make out with this guy."

"What would Saint Patrick say about that?"

"Dude, I so don't care. I am totally drunk. Come down."

I slowly began to assemble myself for a trip to Jamaica Plain. Boston shamrock t-shirt. Boots. The phone rang.

"Hi! I'm Boston Girl's friend. She says to get your ass over here."

"I'm coming. I'm coming. Is she making out with that dude at the bar yet?"

"Hang on. No, no, not yet."

I grabbed a cab and squinted suspiciously at the driver.

"Do you know Boston?"

"Yes," he lied.

"I want to go to Jamaica Plain. Take Harvard Avenue past Beacon and then take a left at Longwood."

"What? Sorry. You talk too fast."

Twenty-five frustrating dollars later, I arrived at James's Gate. I felt like I was on the other side of the moon. But I opened the door of the pub to find a familiar rough-hewn

Irish room full of tables, chairs and noisy people in green. One of them, sporting a huge white and green striped hat, grabbed my arm. It was Boston Girl.

"Dude, I'm so drunk," she announced. "I started drinking at eleven. Have an Irish Black Russian."

She introduced me to the tableful of happy people. One of the men bought me an Irish Black Russian. That's the ticket!

"There's that guy I want to make out with," said Boston Girl.

"Where?"

"Across the table."

I looked across the table and there he was, sitting beside an older middle-aged woman. He had glasses and a goatee and looked to be in his mid-twenties. The woman was wearing a long-sleeved green shirt with a deep V-neck and looked very well preserved. She also looked like the cat who was about to eat the cream.

"So, are you a student?" I yelled at him across the table.

"Yes. I'm doing an MA at Boston U. I'm in Engineering."

"That's great! Boston Girl is at Boston U, too!"

Then I looked at the woman beside him.

"So, are YOU a student?"

There was, perhaps, the tiniest touch of malice in my voice.

"No," she said, demurely.

"She's a student of Life," said the Engineering student.

And right then I knew that Boston Girl had lost her chance to make out.

The older lady was obviously into that young man, and he was drunk enough not to have noticed that she was over fifty. She had big eyes, shimmery hair, and very good skin, lightly freckled and tight as a drum. On a gold chain she wore a pendant that read: **YES I DO.**

I don't remember exactly when they left; I was distracted by the surprise entrance of a pipe band playing, of all things, "Scotland the Brave." But just before that I saw the May-December romance standing by the table, she putting an arm around him, and saying something amusing in his ear. Frankly, he looked rather nervous. He was laughing, but his body language suggested a rabbit caught in the proverbial headlights.

"She was fifty-seven," sighed Boston Girl later.

"How do you know?" I demanded

"She told me. She is divorced. She has two children. Her son is thirty-four."

"Oh my."

"The dude is twenty-six," said Boston Girl. "He told me."

I tried doing the math, gave up, tried again, pondered the result.

"I don't want to be that woman when I am fifty-seven," I said.

"Dude, she looked *great*."

"Yeah, she looked great. But she was divorced and alone

in a bar on St. Patrick's Day, picking up men younger than her children."

I looked forward into my own future and shivered.

"How sad is that?"

Diamond Polishing

I am of two minds about the t-shirt slogan "Leave every man better than you found him." On the one hand, I think it is savvy and cute. It's a nod and a wink to the reality of many Western women's experience. We date a lot of men. We break up with a lot of men. Hopefully, we and the men will remember each other fondly. Hopefully, the men have been transformed by the magical experience of being our boyfriends. We look forward in sisterly solidarity to the women who will come after us. They'll thank us, we imagine, for having domesticated the men just a little more.

On the other hand, it is frightening. It assumes serial monogamy is the natural state of things. Women fall in love, we give a little polish to our diamonds in the rough, we fall out of love, and then forward we go. But it is not as emotionally simple as that. I have found the process quite depressing. It's not that I wish I had married any of my ex-flames. It's that I wish there weren't so many of them. It's difficult work, breaking hearts or having my own heart broken. And, from an economic point of view, that's a lot of hours spent diamond polishing for other women.

One solution is to quit diamond polishing. My friend Lily preaches a gospel of dating detachment and "emotional chastity," and I think she is right. I include in this a refusal to indulge in the feminine pastime of stripping and refurbishing a man as if he were a garage-sale find. Although we should demand good manners and respect from the men we date, we should hold off on giving them personal advice. We should not, for example, go shopping with them. If they dress like a rave kid at the age of forty, or dress like an absent-minded professor at the age of twenty-five, that's their problem. If they love rap or Top 40, it's not our business to open their ears to the beauties of Beethoven or the dark energy of Industrial.

Another solution, of course, is to opt out of girlfriend-hood. This is easier said than done for Searching Singles, who long to get married, but I am suggesting that thirteen times a bride-potential, never a bride. Now, at the ripe old age of thirty-six, I believe I should have realized by the third date with some of my ex-flames that they were a dead loss as future husbands. They would simply take too much polishing, and some had unfixable flaws anyway: alcoholism, atheism, outrageous arrogance. So much work and worry! As I confessed my woes with one happily married friend in Montreal, she exclaimed, "Dottie, relationships are not supposed to be work! They're supposed to be *fun!*"

So I think that is my final position on the postcard. Don't worry about leaving any man better than you found him. Just determine early on if he is good enough for *you.*

Them's the Breaks

It was a beautiful spring day. The sun shone, the breezes breezed, the sky was blue. Harvard, always glamorous, was at its best. Volker and I took a stroll by the elegant Law Library and sat on a sweet curved bench. What could be better, I thought, than to be with Volker on such a gorgeous day? Well, it would have been better if his allergies weren't acting up and making him miserable. But despite that, I was brimming over with contentment. And then he broke up with me.

I was very surprised.

He gave his reasons for the breakup. I thought that they were crazy. I felt deeply sorry for the sudden and even bizarre circumstances that had led to his decision, but they had nothing to do with me. Volker thought differently. And he was adamant. It was over.

Well, a girl just can't argue with that. When a man says it's over, it's over.

"Well, them's the breaks," I said. "I'm going now. I'll e-mail you in a couple of days."

"Are you okay?" asked Volker.

I suppose tact was a bit much to expect from Volker, but I was annoyed all the same.

"I am fine," I snapped.

As I walked away, I heard him say "Sorry!"

So that's that, kids. I know you romantics out there will be sorry. I'm sorry myself. I'm not particularly Seraphic, either. I don't mind not being married—it's a good old life one way or the other—but it was a lot of fun to be Volker's girlfriend. We went on walks around town. We heard a few concerts. We ate a lot of great dinners. We talked about our studies, about history, and even about you guys. I got to practice speaking German. Volker got to improve his English. We admired each other. It was fun.

The great cloud was always what would happen if Volker went back to Germany. And I think now that if I could change anything, I would have refused ever to discuss the future. Sadly, Volker had read a deeply contemptuous article in *Der Spiegel* about the supposed American lust to get married as quickly as possible. On something like our fifth date, he brought up the subject. I hit the ceiling, but it was too late. The M word was out there, and it never went away. I didn't help matters, either, by joking about *The Rules* and airing my courtship theories. In the absence of women friends, I often spoke to Volker as if he were a woman.

All things considered, it was a clean break. To make sure it stayed clean, I refrained from writing about it until I calmed down. My mother, I am sure, will think I should not have written about it at all. However, I feel a need to explain why Volker will disappear from the book. Also, breaking up is pretty common in the Single Life. It helps keep us Single.

A Proper Goodbye

Volker believed he was allergic to my hair. That looks rather silly, out here in print, but there was nothing silly about the rash that kept appearing around his right eye. It itched and it stung. Volker eliminated various allergens from his life until he came to the conclusion that the guilty allergen was me. And, not knowing any better, I went along with this diagnosis. I changed shampoos, I wore my hair in a bun, I covered it with a scarf. However, the rash kept reappearing, and it kept getting worse. So Volker broke up with me on that sunny day two weeks ago outside Harvard Law.

"Look," I said. "I'll cut my hair."

"You will not cut your hair!"

"Well, then, look, I'll give hair to a lab. Let them determine …"

"If we were going to be married, all this would be worth it," said Volker. "But I am not sure about that, and I don't know if I ever will be sure."

And that is when I knew we were breaking up, and shortly thereafter I left. All I could think of, in my shock, was that I had to find a woman to talk to. Women have three stress reactions: fight, flight or complain. I had put up a weak fight, I was now in flight, and I needed to complain. The second I got home to my messy apartment I called Boston Girl.

"Dude, I am marking papers. I have seventy-six grades to turn in by midnight. I'll come as soon as I can."

And that left my ex-Science Guy housemate, who ambled into the kitchen just as I burst in.

"Volker broke up with me," I said.

"Whoa!" said Jon. "Whoa! Was that a surprise or—"

"Yes, of course it was a surprise," I snapped. "It came completely out of left field. I hope I have beer left in the fridge."

"You can have one of mine if you want," said Jon.

"He thinks he's allergic to my hair," I said, getting my beer.

"What? That's crazy," said my housemate.

"Yes, it is," I said.

It had dawned on me that, for a scientist, Volker had taken a very unscientific approach to the matter of my hair. Was my hair a scapegoat? If Volker had wanted to continue in this relationship, we could have worked on the allergy problem together. But I was no mood for a scientific dissection myself. I was committed to pain control. I drank two beers, waited for Boston Girl, skimmed Volker's follow-up e-mail, and listened to Jon read from my copy of *The Girl's Guide to Surviving a Break-up*.

"Okay, listen to this: *He is not the One...I want you to remember one thing: In the simple act of breaking up with you, he has proved himself to NOT be the One for you.* Now, THAT's true. Unh-huh...Hmmm! Now *this* is interesting!"

The author, Delphine Hirsh, and my housemate, Jon, seemed to agree on everything. They definitely agreed that the relationship was over and Volker was never coming back.

As painful as it was, I preferred this approach. It was over. It was a surprise, but it was over. Boston Girl arrived with ice cream, chips and a minority report.

"He'll be back in two days," she said.

"Don't do this to me, Boston Girl. The book says he is gone."

"The book is wrong. This is not a real breakup. I *know* Volker. I saw you together. You were both happy. He looked better when he was with you. Sort of confident and manly. He'll be back in two days."

He was not back in two days. Or three. Or four. Or five. I kept my appointment with my therapist, who wanted to know all about it. Therapist-like, she had neither the pessimism of Delphine Hirsh nor the optimism of Boston Girl. Her professional opinion was that Volker was not allergic to my hair. She suggested that he was scared. And although she saw nothing wrong in my Dignified Silence approach, she said that there was plenty of time for me to decide if I ever wanted to talk to him again. So I left her office and e-mailed him directly.

In the Father Brown mysteries, G.K. Chesterton usually draws a veil over what penitent Catholic crooks have to say to Father Brown and what he has to say to them. I will draw here a similar veil. You may have all written and received similar e-mails, so you can imagine them. The businesslike enquiry. The passionate explanation. The volcanic diatribe followed soon after by a kinder rebuke. The overwrought expression of relief. The concerned query. The suggestion of drinks. And so it was last night that I found myself on my way to drinks with my dear ex-boyfriend Volker.

Providential

There are two ways to finish this story: the self-promoting way and the self-effacing way. Both are factually correct. Artistically, the former might be better.

I could describe the busy Boston street, bright in the setting sun. I could portray Volker, in his mismatched scientist clothes, as a bit of a clown, the tell-tale weal under his eye proving that two weeks away from my hair had not cured him. I could mark the progress of Volker's rash as we drank our beer under the stairs of a sports bar and express how elated I was that it had nothing to do with me. I could tell you I laughed and encourage you to laugh with me. I could detail how, back in the street, I pulled my innocent hair free of its bun. And I could exult that a car stopped and, as Volker stood there, pasty and silent, a handsome man with dreadlocks told me my hair was beautiful.

This is the "You go, girl" ending. This is the Fay Weldon, feminist ending. It's the ending I had in mind when I started the story. From hair allergy to hair glory—isn't that neat? But there's a problem. It's not a Catholic ending. It's sterile. Some guys do dig my hair. So what? As a victory, it's banal. And besides, it's not the best part of the story.

So let's try the other ending then, the self-effacing one. It might not be as arty, but it's even more true. It's wonderful. And like all wonderful endings, it returns to the beginning.

Let's go back under the stairs at the Sunset Grill. Volker and I are sitting on stools at a high table; I'm too short for it. The weal under Volker's eye is darkening. The bass line thumping through the faulty sound system is annoying me, but I push it aside to ask my question. In his most heart-wrenching e-mail, Volker called me his angel. He hinted that I have saved him from some frightful fate, some dark secret that he has never told me about. And now that there is no point in secrets, I want to know what it is.

"Er," says Volker, his eyes sliding away. "It's embarrassing."

"Why do you think I'm here?" I demand.

And as I say it, I know it is true. I'm not here to acquit my hair or, *pace* Boston Girl, get back together with Volker. It's over. We both know it. I'm here to hear a story, the story that will make this all better.

"It isn't much of a story," says Volker, but as he tells it, in rushed half sentences, it turns into a wonderful story. And it turns *this* story into Volker's story, not mine.

Volker had been in America for months. He was lonely. He missed his family, his friends, and the merry beer-drinking culture of student Germany. He did his best to find a Cambridge equivalent. He went on late-night pub crawls with other Europeans. And on one of those nights, a December night, he met an attractive Greek woman. They had a half-hour chat and exchanged e-mail addresses. The next day, the

Greek woman e-mailed him an invitation. And, if Volker understood it correctly, it was an out-of-town booty call.

I have no idea what it is like to be a celibate man. I pass strip joints and feel deeply sorry for the men inside. I read the letters of frustrated "nice guys" to advice columnists and shiver at their fury. I am embarrassed when men are told to be ashamed of being men. But I don't know what it is like to be a lonely, celibate man who has just been propositioned by a sexy woman by e-mail. I think it must be tough. I think it must be tempting.

Volker was tempted. All his life he had held Catholic values mocked by his country and all his friends. But at the moment, they didn't seem like much. Maybe he had been naive. Maybe he was missing out on life. He was a man, and he was lonely. He sat on his couch before his computer and brooded on his new, strange thoughts.

And then he got another e-mail. It was from that cute red-haired girl at church. Which is to say, from me.

"Why on earth do you not ask me out for coffee?" the e-mail demanded.

Volker was stunned. Volker the Scientist would say "Co-incidence." Volker the Catholic turned and looked at God.

"I suppose You think that's funny," he said.

Shaken, he got himself a beer. There was the kind of man who has flings with sirens and the kind of man who has coffee with cute girls from church, he thought. And he remembered which kind he was, and what he really wanted in life. He didn't know if this girl was the wife he wanted, but he knew that what he wanted was not adventures, but a wife.

"That's a good story," I say.

"Err," says Volker.

And as I sit now, on this warm Cambridge river bank, I realize that I am just a bit player in Volker's story. That's okay. I've been a girlfriend many times. It's an old role; I'm slightly typecast. But to discover exactly when I might have been the oblivious tool of Providence—now, that is amazing. By breaking *The Rules*, I inadvertently reminded Volker to keep God's rules.

In every human story, the principals are the hero and God. In every story but my own, the best role I can hope for is female romantic lead. But that's not who I am in Volker's story. And now it's time for me to get off his stage.

Loneliness
Happens

Bitter to Drink

Yesterday was a very happy day indeed. All my stuff and I fit into my brother's tiny car, the music at Mass was fantastic, and there was scarcely any lineup at my favorite Cambridge sandwich shop, Darwin's Ltd. The drive out of Massachusetts, through New Hampshire and Vermont was a cool and pleasant one, and my heart swelled with love as we crossed the border into Canada.

Now I am in my brother's adopted city of Montreal, a seventeenth-century town with a big anglophone minority and block after block of gorgeous old houses and shops. My favorite street, rue St-Denis, is lined with cafés, boutiques and bars. I sat there on a *terrasse* with my brother at "L'Amère à Boire." *L'amère à boire* means "a thing bitter to drink," but the house beer was anything but bitter. It was delicious. When I got back to my brother's house, I thought about the concept of bitterness.

Someone asked me how an older Single can prevent herself/himself from growing bitter and blaming God. I slept on that all night. But first, I lay awake and thought about Job, who demanded justice from God. And Jacob, who may have wrestled with him. And Rebekah, Jacob's mother, who, when her children were struggling within her womb asked, "If this is to be so, what good will it do me!" and, as Genesis records, "She went to consult the LORD" (Genesis 25:22). And I thought that these great heroes were a lot braver than we are. They had no problem arguing and demanding things from God. We are all cheery "Praise & Worship" music and not much Psalms, which run the gamut of responses to God.

I once popped into a church at my undergrad university and heard yelling from within the nave. There was a man in the aisle yelling with all his might at the crucifix. Awed and rather shocked, I beat a hasty retreat. I wasn't sure if I had witnessed terrible impiety or a great faith, a faith that was strong enough to be honest with God and demand, "If it is to be this way, why do I live?"

After all, we are not the slaves of God. Let me repeat that. We. Are. Not. The. Slaves. Of. God. Slavery is antithetical to Christianity. We should obey God not because we are afraid of God, but because we love God. Job crept and crawled and made sacrifices on behalf of his children just in case they might have sinned. It took real hardship to rouse him to another level in his relationship with God. Finally, Job stood on his feet "like a man" and demanded justice from God. And God said, "My servant Job has spoken well of me." And later Jesus said that we were no longer servants, but friends (John 15.15). A real friend will have it out with a friend, rather than let the friendship die.

So is being perpetually single bitter to drink? Certainly, it often is. At moments it is almost impossible to swallow. And who has brewed this bitter drink? Well, it could be you and me and our bad habits, or it could be the extended adolescence of too many men, or it could be a freak of history and the sexual revolution. However, ultimately (let's face it), God has brewed this bitter drink. And so I suggest we go and inquire of him why this is so. And maybe afterward we will discover in our cups not bitterness, but good beer or the best wine.

The Cross Singles Bear

I'm not sure I can provide spiritual reading for Good Friday as well as others can. My family, though devout, is devout in a quiet way. We go to Mass every Sunday. Afterward we critique the homily or giggle over the hymn selections. We do not engage in shared spiritual reflection. We do not have conversations about what Jesus means to us. We do not expound upon the role of the Holy Spirit in our lives, although we occasionally do wonder over the workings of Providence. Thus, I found having to talk about Jesus in spiritual direction very weird. ("My relationship with Jesus …? Uh, fine, I guess.") But it is Good Friday, so I am going to make an attempt. As a bad-tempered anti-Semite on my bus once complained of Good Friday shop closings, "Some Jew dies, and the whole world stops." Yes. Exactly.

On Good Friday we are especially encouraged to join our sufferings to Jesus' and to deposit our burdens at the foot of the cross. I have always felt that by going to Good Friday services we are mysteriously keeping Jesus company as he dies, two thousand years ago. Did Jesus allow himself to know that millions would gather around him, hundreds, thousands of years later, to be with him in his final agony? I am inclined to think not. After all, there was his shocking cry: "My God, my God, why have you forsaken me?" (Matthew 27:45–46). Professional Scripture scholars, when they squabble over what in the Gospels is historical, have a tool called the "Criterion of Embarrassment." In short, if there is an event in the Gospels that was embarrassing to first- and second-century Christians, and yet it was duly recorded, it probably happened that way. Jesus crying out in agony to his Father—that fits the Criterion of Embarrassment.

Jesus' grief didn't say much to nonbelievers about his divinity and the Father's love for him. But it says a lot to us, particularly to perpetually single people. It tells us that Jesus was, at that moment, earth-shatteringly lonely. He was so lonely, he who was one with the Father felt abandoned by the Father. And although we don't know what that could have meant for Jesus, we sure know what it means for us.

The cross of the unmarried: Loneliness—3 AM loneliness, 11 PM I-can't-face-my-empty-bed loneliness. The loneliness of Friday night when you are all dressed up and have nowhere to go. The loneliness of having a friend bail on a movie because "he" finally called. The loneliness of boring weddings, and the loneliness after fun weddings. The loneliness after a wonderful afternoon visiting married friends with children. The loneliness of Valentine's Day. The loneliness of Christmas parties. The loneliness of New Year's Eve. The loneliness of going to a dance class alone. The loneliness of listening to a humming fridge in the dark.

It is not good for man to be alone, says Genesis. That much is certain. Monks and nuns usually live in communities, so they are not alone the way a single person is alone. They have made their decision. Usually, we have made none, or at least no positive ones. We make negative decisions: "I cannot marry that one." "Well, she doesn't want me, so I won't make a fuss." "He'll never marry me. I'd better cut my losses." These decisions are tinged with sadness and disappointment. The fridge hums relentlessly on.

I have done some stupid things out of loneliness. Dating men from work—well, that was okay, but dating atheists was demoralizing. Dating an alcoholic just because he was a cute, intelligent Catholic—that was pretty dumb. Dating a sleazy, vicious actor just because I hadn't been on a date in years—that was a very bad decision.

I've done some dangerous things out of loneliness, too. I've walked dark streets to get away from myself and my empty apartment. I have gone to nightclubs alone just to lose myself in the music, the crowd, the alcohol. I have let a near-stranger crash on my couch. (We had a mutual friend, but still.)

And I have done some embarrassing things out of loneliness. Read personal ads. Joined Internet dating services. Gone on blind dates made through the Internet. Gone—alone—to dance classes. Tried to get back together with boyfriends I had dumped, or who had dumped me.

Fill in your own personal humiliations, my dear fellow Singles.

Although I never lost my faith in God after my bad marriage, I was very angry at him. Furious. After all, I had been a Good Girl and had not deserved all this crap. I did not deserve all the pain, the humiliation, the temptation, the disappointment and the loneliness. I marched into church one week to give him a piece of my mind. Perhaps it was for all of us, dear Singles, all of us who watch and wait and hope and despair, who climb into our cold beds and listen to the damn fridge hum and the building creak and the branches tap on the window.

"You don't know what it is like to be human," I accused God. "You don't know what it's like to suffer!"

Then my eye fell on the crucifix. And in my heart, I heard him say, "Oh, yes, I do."

Jesus voluntarily took on our suffering along with our humanity, and because he was utterly alone on the cross, we can never be truly alone in our loneliness.

Scars

If we are lucky, the struggles and disappointments of our lives do not show up on our faces. They say that at twenty-five, you have the face that God gave you, but that at forty-five, you have the face that you deserve. I don't believe that. When I worked for a government agency, I had to give support checks to psychiatric patients and crack addicts. I saw a lot of ravaged faces. And our clients didn't deserve those faces; those faces were carved onto them. One of my clients was the mother of a girl whose murder had been front-page news. This woman was a wreck. A complete wreck. She didn't deserve her face.

But most of us privileged, middle-class people in good physical health do not carry our emotional scars on our faces. Some of us might not have any such scars, being unusually gifted at acceptance or covered with spiritual Teflon. But some of us are sensitive souls who never forget a slight or a harm. I imagine our spiritual hearts made flesh, like depictions of the Sacred Heart of Jesus or the Immaculate Heart of Mary, crisscrossed with scars and gouges. Some may resemble a public ice rink at the end of the day: greyish, covered in frost, carved by a hundred blades. They aren't pretty sights. Sensible people are very careful not to show their scarred heart to the wrong people because a recoil or rejection would add its own bitter mark, send up its own spray of ice or blood.

So what do we do, we sensitive souls? We want to be "fully

accepted" and we don't want to hide who we are. But what if who we are includes a heart as pitted as a hockey rink? Well, I'll tell you what *The Rules* has to say about that: "Don't open up too fast" (Rule #19) and "Be honest but mysterious" (Rule #20). Of your crush object, Ellen Fein and Sherrie Schneider write, "He should always feel that he's in love with the woman of his dreams, not someone damaged." But on the other hand, "don't, as some women do, surprise him with these skeletons after you're married." Somewhere in there, you are allowed, nay, *instructed,* to reveal "whatever truths about yourself you need to share." Tough call.

The Rules puts a lot of stock in a declaration of love as the moment in which you are now allowed to be you. I do not. My goodness. The men to whom I have said "I love you"! I am afraid I have thereby left my own skate marks. And the only ex-boyfriend I keep up with is the one I told straight up, "I don't love you, and if you tell me that you love me, I won't believe you. So don't." He was a little stunned by this, and wasn't sure whether he should be angry or impressed. He decided to go with impressed.

It was a darned honest, if rocky, relationship. I saw his scars; he saw my scars. We addressed each other by our surnames. We insulted each other in two languages. He once smacked me; I once threw a stapler at him. We laughed like lunatics, but there were few illusions and very little romance. He complained after we saw *The Titanic*: he thought it terrible that Leonardo Di Caprio had sacrificed himself for Kate

Winslet. Complain, complain. I got the message. We soon went our separate ways.

So this leads me to my morning's question: who should see our scars? Can we keep our boyfriends or girlfriends only through concealment? Can we be honest only with those men and women with whom there is little hope of a future? Should we present only a perfect image of ourselves, wrapped in tissue, or should we demand complete honesty from the first, and make our lovers into battle buddies? Do we want to be perfect and pretty Kate Winslet, placed on a floating pedestal, or are we willing to risk freezing to death in the North Atlantic of the heart?

Fear of the Red, White and Pink

It is not far away—that fatal day, that day with the power to cast Searching Singles into abject gloom and to rattle the most seraphic of Seraphic Singles, that day that crushes the joy out of men who love and rarely fails to disappoint the women who love them. Yes, my friends, Valentine's Day is upon us again.

The Bollandists, having applied the historical-critical method to St. Dorothy with great success, did it to various other saints, including St. Valentine, whose day was taken away and given to Saints Cyril and Methodius. Catholics no longer call Valentine's Day *Saint* Valentine's Day, although I have seen part of the saint's skull in an isolated church in the Rhineland, and the priest swore up and down that it truly belonged to St. Valentine.

So much for history. It is the present or, rather, the near future that concerns us. The public streets, the private markets are already awash with the red, white and pink. Valentine-themed articles are appearing in newspapers across the western world. The front shelves of T.J. Maxx are full of lurid pink lingerie. The price of roses is skyrocketing. Restaurateurs are laying in stocks of champagne and truffle oil, giggling over how much money they will rake in next week. Valentine's Day, as any man could tell you, is a license to steal. Be prepared.

Singles without swains, do not allow yourselves to feel like leftover Christmas cake on Valentine's Day. Start planning now. Make a date with other Singles. Get dinner reservations at a place without a Valentine's Day surcharge, or throw an anti–Valentine's Day party. If, foolishly, you have limited yourself to friends with special friends, rent a stack of comforting movies and buy some snacks. Invite relatives over. Avoid the bars because they will be packed with the predatory. These will be either desperate themselves for love or snuffling the ground for the scent of your own desperation. If you are truly miserable, get you to church. Have a conversation with St. Anne, whose job it is to find women a husband: "*St. Anne, St. Anne, send me a man.*" I am not sure whose job it is to find men wives. St. Joseph? "*St. Joe, St. Joe, send me a —.*"Hmm…Boys, make up your own rhyme.

As for you Singles with swains, do not, I beg you, make too much of this day. The only way to remain serene is to expect nothing. My best Valentine's Day was the only Valentine's Day I ever was surprised beyond all expectations. My sisters and I were given surprise chocolate—by our dear old dad. Expect nothing, and whatever your poor beleaguered sweetie gives you will be as manna in the desert. And incidentally, your femininity will not be forever in question if you give *him* something nice. A book, perhaps. A paperweight. A good pen. Nothing with hearts on it, although a plastic model of a real heart might be cool, if your swain is a medical student or a Goth.

And as for you male Singles, you have my deepest sympathies. *She's* not after your wallet—the florist, the restaurant and the jewelry store are. That's not her fault. That's not your fault. But the facts of life mean that you have to give your girlfriend *something*. If you are absolutely broke, that something is going to be a romantic candlelit dinner in your well-scrubbed kitchen, with poetry reading. Not *your* poetry—Gerard Manley Hopkins, pray for us! Download Shakespeare's sonnets from the Internet, find ones that apply, and practice reading them in advance. And make a valentine out of red and white paper: so much better than the stupid ones in the stores. Don't sweat the roses. No truly nice woman would make a poor man pay $100 for something that the rest of the year costs no more than $50. But as for you men with cash…

The Silent Valentines

My dear fellow Singles, both Seraphic and Searching, the fatal V-Day is upon us. Like you, I have mixed feelings about this day. And like many of you I am not going out to a restaurant tonight to eat the romantic but overpriced *prix fixe* dinner. But my feelings are nothing compared to those of certain other women. Indeed, this piece is dedicated to my friend Red and her mother, for Red's father died recently, leaving Red's mother a widow, if I may use that term. "We don't use the W-word," says Red.

I am not sure how to address the newly single status of women who have lost the loves of their lives to death. This is beyond my experience: a lot has happened in the great kaleidescope of my dating life, but I have never been widowed. There have been no deaths. My dead include my grandparents, my uncle and a dear teacher. But no beloveds.

My grandmother Gladys lost her husband when she was only sixty. I am told that she couldn't cope at all, but also that my first sister, born the next week or so, was a great consolation to her. Before she died, Grandma told me a little about her relationship with my grandfather. There were ups and downs. "But I was his *Lady*," said my grandmother, smiling. She lived as a widow for twenty-six years. Both my mother and my grandmother kept my grandfather's memory green for me. And I am grateful that I know him through them.

Then there was a college friend, a month or two pregnant, whose twenty-five-year-old husband collapsed and died of a heart attack while playing floor hockey. He was a good man, a devout Catholic, an article-writing law student, full of promise. The church was packed at the funeral, and it was a large church. The widow was a pillar of calm. I was not at the gravesite, but I am told that she gave the eulogy herself: she counseled the mourners to accept the will of God. I don't know what to make of that. Shock? Old Canadian Stiff Upper Lip *par excellence*? A deep faith beyond my shallow understanding? The baby was a boy; she named him for his father.

And there is a more recent friend, a wonderful, warm woman, a chaplain, who went through a terrible divorce but then found love with an older man. They married; he died. The ex still lives, and I think, "How unfair!"

A very dear friend married a man much older than she, and she knows that in all likelihood he will go first. As she told me this thought, she seemed somehow anchored by its gravity. And I thought, if you fall in love, a heart will one day be broken. When you fall in love, either someone will fall out of love, or someone will die. Joy and pain are hand in hand.

I am a Christian, so I believe that those who love will be reunited. I don't have anything more to say than that. Sometimes it is better to be silent before great love and great grief. So I will merely offer my sympathy to all widows who read this and say how strongly I believe that "Death shall have no dominion."

On the Just and Unjust

Last night I went to a little reunion dinner of high school friends. We have dinner together quite regularly, although either C or I am usually missing. (C works many night shifts, and I've been abroad.) Our high school was an all-girls' Catholic school with an old and proud tradition; we congratulate ourselves on having gone there. It certainly helped to make us, for good and ill, who we are today.

We all have quite different lives. N is an engineer and the married mother of three little girls. Smiley works in an office and is the recently separated mother of two girls, one tall and one small. J is a science teacher who got engaged this August. C is a nurse in a neonatal ward and has never married. I, well, you know all about me. Our differences mean that we always have a lot to talk about, and there is always something new. This time there was Smiley's new apartment to tour, N's new baby to play with, and J's new engagement ring to examine. Neither N nor I knew that J was engaged, so we both shrieked happily at the news.

After dinner, Smiley mentioned that she had found other girls in our graduating class on Facebook. And thus we all trooped off to her teenage daughter's room to look them up. In most cases, these were women we had not seen in seventeen years. Most of them were not our friends. In fact, they had belonged to what I suppose you could call the "fast set." Some had bullied us or our weaker friends, smoked cigarettes in the washroom, and gone off on March Break to Quebec City to hold nameless orgies. Some of them had worn "rocker chick" makeup and dated boys we never saw. Perhaps we sometimes saw their cars blaring music, idling outside the convent that was our school. At least one of this set did not go on to postsecondary education after graduation; she became a check-out girl. As she had scared the living daylights out of me in ninth grade, I thought that was justice.

Well! Through the magic one-way mirror of a computer screen, the faithful remnant of my crowd stared at pictures of *her* reunited crowd. Whereas we have quietly merry reunion suppers, just as in school we had quietly merry lunches, her crowd has loud parties featuring much alcohol and breast implants. The party pictures show the women we remember, only looking much, much older, and showing less leg and way more breast.

"We don't look that bad, do we?" exclaimed J, N and Smiley.

"We wear sunblock," I said. "You must wear sunblock, J. Do you?"

J nodded.

I looked again at the screen, and we marveled at their leathery complexions. It was easy to imagine that they had just kept on with their cigarettes, their alcohol, their tanning habits and their nameless orgies. But, guess what? Those were just the party pictures. In their Facebook profile photos, the women were quite different.

In the Facebook profile photos, they were women with little children. They were women with double-barreled or unfamiliar surnames. They were married. I looked at one woman I remembered as being particularly unpleasant and who had, I always felt, a face like an elephant's toe.

"She has two children, a really cute husband, and a house in Leaside," said Smiley.

And that news struck me in the tenderest place in my heart. Girls I had vaguely considered ill-mannered, immoral or kind of dumb had won the social lottery. They had husbands. They had children. They even had houses in Leaside or other nice places to raise children. I had none of those things. Suddenly, I felt very, very tired. I felt the same kind of exhaustion I have at other parties, when people ask me how I like my studies in Boston. Leaving the knot of beloved women at the computer, I lay down on Smiley's daughter's bed and rested.

On the way home, sensible J reminded me that I knew nothing about those women's lives. A Facebook photo wasn't enough to tell me if they were satisfied in their marriages or with their kids, or what their living circumstances truly were. And this is true. Very true. It is also true that I may have underestimated the girls who sat at the back of the classrooms and made so much noise in the halls. I was always, despite my inability to subtract fractions, an intellectual snob. Maybe they were nicer than they appeared or became nicer later. And of course I know that it is not always the brainy girls, the witty girls, the truly self-confident girls who get snapped up right away. J herself, who is a wonderful, caring, independent and intelligent soul, a model of our high school's ideal woman, is proof of this fact: she will be married for the first time at thirty-six.

I won't be remarried by thirty-seven, of course, and Smiley will cease to be married. Although my own singlehood doesn't usually faze me, last night I felt overcome by a cloud of regret. *It isn't fair*, I thought. But then my long theological and religious training kicked in, and I remembered part of the King James' version of what Jesus said on the subject. Here's the whole:

> *Ye have heard that it hath been said, Thou shalt love thy neighbor, and hate thine enemy. But I say unto you, Love your enemies, bless them that curse you, do good to them that hate you, and pray for them which despitefully use you, and persecute you; That ye may be the children of your Father which is in heaven: for he maketh his sun to rise on the evil and on the good, and sendeth rain on the just and on the unjust* (Matthew 5:43–45).

A Scraped Elbow

They say redheads bruise more easily than other people. I think I do. Sometimes I catch sight of a new bruise in the shower and think, *Now where did that come from?* I seem to get cut and bruised without noticing it until after the event. For example, somehow I cut my elbow at the schoolyard where I took my nephew on Saturday night. I'm not sure how it happened. The most likely opportunity was when I crouched under a small hanging bar to show Pirate how to hang and, when my arms were both in the air, he clambered on my lap.

"Swing," said Pirate before tumbling heavily off into the gravel.

I let go to catch him and fell heavily myself. But I didn't have time to think of that. My nephew had fallen on his shoulder and rubbed it meditatively. As usual, he didn't cry.

"Pirate," I scolded. "You have to be more careful!"

"I don't think men mean to be mean," I told a friend over the phone. "I think they just say things without realizing how they sound."

"Oh, I think men know how to be mean," said my friend. "My ex-boyfriend was the meanest person I ever met."

I was sitting on the kitchen floor under the phone. Some

man had said something terribly mean earlier that evening without seeming to realize how terribly mean it was. It was call-up-the-therapist mean.

"I think most of them do not know how they sound. They just kind of blunder around," I said.

We changed the subject. My friend is studying abroad, thousands of miles from home. She is dating one of the locals, and she has to decide soon if she is going to stay in his country or not. She's stressed.

"I haven't been following *The Rules*," she confessed.

I caught the note of fear, and I felt fear, too. I love this woman, and I don't want her to get hurt. Of course, this is not heaven, so she's going to get hurt anyway. But the whole point to following *The Rules* is not creating more hurt for yourself than you're otherwise going to get.

"Maybe you should," I said. "Look what happened to me."

"I *know*," said my friend.

Worldwide, my friends knew that I was breaking *The Rules*, and some of them reminded me that we had a *Rules* pact. Corny as it might sound, my last breakup only cemented our faith in *The Rules*.

"And you can't let him think you are staying only because of him. That is *death*."

"I know."

"If he says, *I hope you're not staying just because of me*, it's over. I mean," I said. "Look what happened to *me*."

"I know."

Twenty-two years of dating, eleven breakups. That's a lot of disappointment. It takes its toll. Twenty-two years of: "*If I catch you with another man, I'll kill you*"; "*How Catholic are you?*"; "*I'm an atheist*"; "*What I really want is a nice Jewish woman doctor*"; "*Your friends are either religious maniacs or moral degenerates*"; "*I can't do long-distance*"; "*I'm sorry, he's not at home.*" To tell you the truth, my psyche feels rather banged up. I wish now that I hadn't dated so much. I know a woman who found the love of her life even before she left her nasty husband. Actually, I know two women like that: the other was my great aunt. Why not me?

My one stress-free dating relationship (three dates, no kiss) was with a handsome commitmentphobe at home here in Canada last year. I suspected that he liked dating a woman who usually lived in Boston. We ate delicious expensive dinners that he paid for and flirted outrageously, as if it all didn't matter. Indeed, it *didn't* matter.

"No spark," I told my friends.

We agreed it was a shame. He is awfully good looking and witty. But on the bright side, I was never disappointed. The whole thing was just a social experiment without any expectations. I haven't noticed any bruises. It was a nice change.

In the schoolyard, I realized that my elbow was stinging. I looked at it and, sure enough, a little disc of soft flesh had been torn away.

"I've cut my elbow," I told my nephew.

He look concerned, which was touchingly advanced for a two-year-old.

"Did somebody hurt you?" he asked.

"No, honey," I said. "I hurt myself."

Growing Old Alone

The morning after my friend Melanie's birthday, I was not a pretty sight. Moppets of twentysomething can do the "stay-up-till-2" thing and look fantastic, but not I. I tottered out of the kitchen and caught a glimpse of myself in Lily's mirror. Those darned old lines—usually unnoticeable—were etched into my face from nose to chin. I returned with an announcement.

"I'm middle-aged!"

"What brought this on?" asked Lily. She was making pancakes and frowning at the scrambled eggs, which looked gloppy.

"I don't know. I walked into the kitchen a young person, and then when I left I was middle-aged!"

"You won't be middle-aged until you're forty," said Lily. "No, actually, you won't be middle-aged until you're forty-five."

"Hmm," I said. I didn't feel like arguing with that.

This morning, though, I have been thinking about age again because I woke up with a toothache. My tooth with the newly canaled root was complaining. There's nothing like a toothache to make me think about *Anno Domini*. I have a few grey hairs, but they are much more subtle. But my next thought was, well, at least I am home in Canada.

When I was much younger, my mother told me that I should marry a man before he turned thirty. "After thirty they do not change," she warned. "They are set in their ways." She married my father when he was twenty-nine and, presumably, still flexible. This maternal advice makes me wonder if I should *ever* marry again. After all, I am now thirty-six and rather set in my ways. There are definite changes that come with marriage, including having to share a bed, sacrifice time with my family to spend time with an alien family, budget, shop for groceries regularly, iron shirts, make the orange juice and face a whole list of uncomfortable possibilities. I mean, all this was one thing for my mother to get used to. She was, what? Twenty-three? But I am thirty-six and—being home again—I quite like my single life.

The usual fear the perpetually single have is of growing old alone. But, thanks to the excellent planning of my parents, it is very unlikely that I will grow old alone. They furnished me with four spritely younger brothers and sisters, and no child ever had a better present. My ex-husband once decried this bounty and told me that if my parents had fewer children I, like him, could have had the advantages of skiing lessons, top-notch dance classes and horses. Only the Catholic distaste for divorce prevented me from leaving him there and then. *Skiing lessons.*

So not only do I have these super brothers and sisters who (I hope and pray) will survive me, I have a nephew and, as of September, a brand-new sister-in-law. Yay! Now that is one wedding in which I will dance with feather-light feet. She's an investment in my old-lady future. Hooray!

So there is my answer to the problem of growing old alone. And it is a problem: the women of my family are tremendously long-lived. There are probably, alas, many tooth surgeries ahead of me in this life. I grow old, I grow old, I shall wear my trousers rolled (T.S. Eliot). But, thanks to my parents and also to my partner-attracting siblings, I will not do so alone.

As for you Single readers, if you don't have a family you can stand, I heartily suggest that you either salvage those members you might be able to tolerate or attach yourself to a new family, as a sort of all-purpose courtesy aunt or uncle.

When You Least Expect It

One evening in our blue-and-orange-plaid dining room, my parents made a joke at the expense of their tiny children.

"I wish I could fly," I must have said.

"You can fly," said my parents. "These are flying chairs. If you sit in them and wish hard enough, they will fly."

"Really?"

We were thrilled.

"Yes, but the most important thing is that when you wish, you must not think about white elephants."

Argh! Try as I might, whenever I tried to will the chairs into flight, I couldn't help but think of white elephants. And this reminds me of kindly married people who assure single people that they'll find that special someone when they least expect it. When you are longing to find that special someone, you are living permanently in a state of hopeful expectation.

The best retort to the question "Why are you single?" was made by Mae West, who said, "Because I was born that way." But to tell you the truth, I can't remember the last time someone asked me that question. My grandmothers have died, and I have no aunts. When my mother last alluded to the subject, I delicately mentioned my early divorce. Two of my writing students, a delightful Hindu couple, may have asked, for I remember them telling me that marriages are made in heaven and there is someone for everyone.

There are times when being single is acutely painful. Big, boring weddings where you don't know any guests except your own unmarried sisters, and you are all falling into a bog of spinster depression. Bridal showers, with their dumb games and pastel plates. And, worst of all for me, age thirty-six, baby showers.

I've had boyfriends, and I've even had the big white dress, but a baby I do not have. A baby I may never have. And I love babies—at least, the babies my family produces. Thus it is a special kind of torture to find myself in a parlor with a gang of women, a third of them pregnant or holding babies, listening to baby chat for three hours or more. But of course all of these events are not about *me* and *my* feelings of hurt and loss but about the Bride or the New Mom, so I do my best to soldier through. The time to fall apart is on the way home, either in private or with other single and childless friends. The only polite answer to a fellow guest's "So, honey, anyone yet?" is "Not yet, but here's hoping!"

"That's the spirit," your torturer may say. "You know what, you'll find somebody when you least expect it."

"I am sure you are right," you lie. "There's someone for everyone, right?"

Snappy comebacks are rude and come across as bitter. Save them for mothers and aunts. Mine is, "I *was* married, and I didn't like it much."

It astonishes me that nowadays, when Western women have more freedom and economic opportunities than ever before, we are still obsessed with finding someone special. We can do anything. We can be anything. We have fantastic models of independent women: Dorothy Day, Ayaan Hirsi Ali, Louisa May Alcott, most of the women in the Calendar of Saints. So why do we beat ourselves over the head with our own interrogation: *Why am I single?* And why do we spend our hard-earned money on dating services and Internet sites? Some of those memberships are very expensive. Wouldn't it make more sense to spend the money on a health club or a service trip to El Salvador or something else with tangible results?

My advice to Searching Singles everywhere is to give up the search. Give up. Let go and let God. If you are under twenty, you are too young to be worrying about this anyway. Today has its own worries. If you are over twenty, worry is not going to bring you a spouse. Focus on something else: excelling in school, enjoying your career, improving society, developing the relationships you have with your family and friends. Become so busy you can't go to all the weddings and showers to which you are invited. Send a lovely gift. You don't have to go personally; your gift can go for you. (And the bride/new mom will save money on your meal.) Giving up doesn't mean despair. It means freeing yourself from despair. It means grasping the tranquility of "Maybe I'll marry, and maybe I won't. But meanwhile, God thinks I'm fabulous."

It's a big beautiful world out there. Don't sit around missing out because you're single. There are people to meet and things to see. There are adventures aplenty. Go out and get them.

Other People's Children

Running Away to Home

When I was first engaged, my fiancé and I came up with what we thought was an ingenious solution to the Christmas problem: on Christmas Eve, he would go home to his family and I would go home to mine. We reasoned that this would have to be renegotiated that distant day when we had children, but for now our decision was a testament to how much smarter we were than anyone else in our marriage-preparation class.

I knew that Christmas as a married lady would bring some changes. For instance, my mother got a Christmas stocking until she was married. Since my mother is all about tradition, I realized that my Christmas-stocking days would be over. And I knew I would have obligations toward 'my fiancé's family. Their principal Christmas Eve tradition was not Midnight Mass, but dinner at a chain Chinese buffet restaurant. The year I was married, they also planned to go to a late Christmas Eve service at an Anglican church to hear my then-husband sing in the choir. I made it clear that I could not join them in this, for I wanted to go to Midnight Mass at the cathedral of my home city. However, the Chinese restaurant was not far from a train station, and I calculated I could take a train to my city and get there in time.

The Chinese buffet was mediocre, but my new family enjoyed it immensely. I remember this dinner as a fun occasion. But as it became time for me to leave, my in-laws cajoled me to put aside my plans to go home, to stay with them and then go on to the Anglican church to hear my husband sing. I explained that I wanted to go to Midnight Mass. They objected. I insisted that I *needed* to go to Midnight Mass. Their objections became more forceful. My then-husband tried to persuade me himself. But in the end, my brother-in-law drove me to the train station, and I believe I left my then-husband and in-laws in a bad humor. I myself was slightly shaken. I felt as if I had fought a decisive battle.

It was an icy cold Canadian night. I walked for half an hour from the train station to the cathedral, shivering but flushed with the satisfaction of my stubborn victory. I was late, but I had missed only the procession. The cathedral was packed, and I squeezed in among the other latecomers in the back, standing on my frozen toes to get a momentary glimpse of my beloved priest. His soft Glaswegian voice sounded a welcome throughout the church, and I thanked God.

After Mass, I struggled home to my parents' house. I let myself in and went downstairs to the living room. My family's stockings were hung by the empty fireplace. I lay down on the couch and fell asleep. In the morning, I was awakened by my siblings piling into the living room and exclaiming. All the stockings were gone. In their place were five sets of new slippers, stuffed with chocolates, nuts and clementines. And one set—beyond all my expectations—was labeled for me.

This is the happiest Christmas memory of my life. From this story it is probably clear to you that I was still a child when I married. True: I confess it. It may have been the principal argument for my annulment. But to me this story signifies that, no matter what, I am forever my parents' child, and that the family I already have will always be mine.

It's Great Not to Date

Over Sunday brunch at the Deli, my mother slid the parish bulletin across the table to me.

"Look," she said, "there's a singles' group!"

And I had been so happy, eating corned beef hash while watching my nephew chew chicken fingers! I glanced at the parish bulletin. The singles' group was "the largest of its kind" and encompassed the entire diocese. There were the usual threats of sports and outings.

"Mom! This is not really a group for Singles; it is a disguised dating club!"

"So?"

"So I don't want to date! I like staying at home with you and Dad."

Mom glanced at Dad. Is it me, or did they look decidedly glum?

All this reminds me of when I was in high school, and Mom worried that I was not spending enough time with "my peers."

"But I don't wanna hang out with my peers!"

Mom looked cross. I joined the school pro-life movement. My peers and I narrowly evaded arrest when we were not, in fact, being arrested. I remember standing in front of a paddy wagon as it took my friends away. It screeched to a halt. My peers wondered what was going on, and looked through the bars to the front window. "It's Dorothy!" they cheered. A nice mustachioed police officer came out and gave me a caution. If I didn't move, he'd arrest me. Well, I wasn't afraid of jail, but I was afraid of what my dad would say if I ended up there, so I moved. Anyway, back to dating.

I ended my dating career on a high note, I think. Of course, I was greatly annoyed with having been broken up with. That still seems wrong. The universe is now out of order. But the guy who broke up with me was exactly the kind of guy I hoped to meet in Boston: a practicing Catholic who was good at math and science. Good men are hard to find, but I found one. Mission accomplished. That we broke up is immaterial. I returned home victorious.

As it happens, my dating life ended none too soon. I get very tired in the evenings now, and besides, I have to be home by 6:30 to make dinner for my parents. Dinner is at seven. Then I do the dishes. The last thing I want to do after that is get ready to go out. Meanwhile, I see as many people as I like: my friends, my editors, my students, theology profs, nuns. Conversation flows easily with all these people. There are no awkward moments, fears or uncertain expectations. Of course, I never see movies in the cinema any more. I simply cannot afford them, or when I can, I cannot make myself pay the $12 charge. Twelve dollars! What madness.

Moreover, just as the latest movie is not worth $12, it is not worth the trouble of dating. Dating is a ridiculous modern invention anyway. I think nostalgically of those nineteenth-century days when nice young men addressed themselves to a young lady's mother after church, and she invited them to call. The young lady didn't have to go any farther than the parlor. The gentleman didn't have to spend any more than the price of flowers or, for the greatly daring, candy. I met my last ex-boyfriend at church. I highly recommend it.

Der Gute and the Bear

1

It was on such a brilliant sunny day as this when I first met Der Gute. I was standing in a cafeteria luncheon line in a small college in Germany, trying to match the words on the menu overhead to the steaming foodstuffs underneath. It was my third day there, so I wasn't exactly fluent. I pretended that the students behind me were deaf.

"*Guten Tag. Ich möchte…*uh…*die Bratkartoffeln…und…*uhhh …*Was is das*?"

"*Gemüse.*"

"*Ja*, okay, *Gemoosuh*," I said, comprehending *nicht*. "*Und auch der Wurst. Danke schön.*"

I sighed with relief. Once again, I would not starve.

The very tall, very thin, very blond and very young man beside me suddenly addressed me in English.

"Excuse me," he said, "Do you know Regis College?"

There, thousands of miles from home, I heard the name of my beloved old Canadian school.

"How on *earth* did you guess?"

The young man's huge blue eyes goggled shyly at me through his glasses, but his mouth twitched with mirth.

"Your pin," he said.

For I was wearing my old school pin, and let that be a lesson to you girls. If you want to meet nice young men in Europe, wear your old Catholic-college pins. My college is not exactly world famous, but as it happened, Der Gute, as we will now call him, had registered to spend his year abroad there. And so began a beautiful friendship—or, at least, an amusing courtesy aunthood.

Der Gute had never spoken to a foreign student in his life, let alone a strange woman. I can only assume he was prompted entirely by the working of the Holy Spirit, who wanted me to feel more at home in Germany and Der Gute to feel more at home in Canada. The major difference is that

I have a large and friendly crowd of friends in Canada who immediately clasped Der Gute to their collective bosom. Der Gute, being shy, awkward, quirky and coddled, has only a family, and you don't get to meet family in Germany for a long, long time. However, I did enjoy our conversation sessions: he listened to me read increasingly simple German books, and I drilled Canadian social norms into his head.

Having taken up watching soccer, I doubted that German standards of masculinity were up to Canadian snuff. For one thing, in soccer grown men sit on the field, pretend that they are hurt and even cry. This would never fly in Canada, and so I told Der Gute in the sunlit empty cafeteria.

"So if I fall down, I cannot cry," said Der Gute, mouth twitching.

"Absolutely not."

"What if I hurt myself very, very badly?"

"You still can't cry. In fact, you have to pretend that you are *less* hurt than you are."

"But what if my mother dies?"

"Well, then you can cry, but only by yourself. Or maybe with a female friend. As long as she doesn't tell anyone afterwards."

"I am so worried," sighed Der Gute. It became either his mantra or his punchline. I've never been quite sure one way or the other.

2

In retrospect, I don't know why I tried to frighten Der Gute into appropriately masculine behavior. After all, he was going into a Canadian college, not the Canadian military. It might have been because my girlfriends back home were looking forward to the cute new foreign student I'd promised. But I suspect Der Gute, with his pale, thin looks and silly jokes, also brought out my maternal side. Although I knew that his age made him safe forever from the violence of the schoolyard, I worried all the same. As did he. About everything.

When I got back to Canada, we sent a flurry of anxiety-driven e-mails back and forth about his arrival. Our friend Stefan was pressuring him into going into his Canadian fraternity. Der Gute did not want to go into the fraternity. I did not want him to go into the fraternity either. I thought if he did, the brothers would duct tape him to a wall. We arranged that he would stay in a monastery until the university residences opened. And on the day of his arrival, I went with a religious to pick him up from the airport. Der Gute was all smiles and luggage. A teddy bear poked out of his backpack.

"This is my bear," he said.

"So I see."

"I never go anywhere without my bear. He would have been very angry at me if I had left him behind."

"Indeed."

"My aunt says that she doesn't mind if I marry you, as long as she's invited to the wedding."

"*What?!*"

I left for Boston the next day.

"He will be a looker when he's thirty," I promised Lily over the phone. "Tall! Blond! Thin! And look at those shoulders. When he fleshes out a bit, he'll be gorgeous."

"I think he's interested in *you*," said Lily.

"He'll get over it. I am too old for him. There's a $50 gift certificate to H&M for anyone who takes him off my hands. Spread the word."

I checked in periodically to see how my protégé was fitting in. Lily was a bit testy. Kelly was still highly amused.

"So, is anyone dating Der Gute yet?"

"Dorothy, Der Gute is *twelve*."

"Not legally."

"Dorothy," yelled Lily. "He has a *teddy bear*."

"It could be a German thing."

And, indeed, when Der Gute came to Boston for a visit, he brought his teddy bear.

"He would have been so angry if I had left him."

3

Some time after Der Gute and his bear went back across the border, I met Volker. Volker was certainly a contrast to Der Gute. Whereas Der Gute was tall, blond and thin, Volker was shorter, brown-haired and slightly squashy. Der Gute had huge, myopic blue eyes; Volker had small, all-seeing grey eyes. Der Gute chattered so quickly, his words crashed into each other like cars in a highway pile-up. Volker preferred silence leavened with a little small talk. Der Gute shrieked; Volker growled. They were obviously two very different men. Nevertheless, I put Volker to the test.

"Did you do your military service?"

"No. Civil. I worked in a youth center."

Bzzzzt. Wrong answer. What kind of young man, I've often wondered, would pass up a mandated, short-term job driving tanks, shooting very expensive guns, and crawling around in the grass covered in war paint? And yet, of the young German men I've met, almost all avoided their mandatory military service by taking the civil-service option. What must Otto von Bismarck be thinking as he looks down from purgatory? He might have had to watch the twentieth-century German nightmare and now this, the death rattle of German military traditions. I suppose the rest of us should be grateful for the last bit, but still.

"Indeed," I said.

"I didn't see the use of military service. I never dreamed Germany would ever be involved in a war again."

"No, indeed."

"I was astonished when war broke out in Yugoslavia."

"Yes."

Some time later, I went home with Volker for a drink. He had a furnished flat near one of Cambridge's more eclectic squares. Apart from the landlady's knick-knacks and a single crucifix, the rooms were free of decoration. There were a few copies of *Scientific American* here and a volume (in German) by Benedict XVI there. Enshrined on a shelf was a bottle of single-malt Scotch. All in all, it seemed a very masculine apartment. But I had to be sure.

"Any bears?" I asked.

"What?"

"You know, stuffed animals. Teddy bears. Elephants."

"No," said Volker.

He did not seem pleased, so I explained about Der Gute.

"I thought it was a German-man thing," I concluded brightly.

"It is not a German-man thing," said Volker.

"Are you sure? Because now all my friends in Canada think that it must be a German-man thing because of Der Gute."

"I think I will have a word with Der Gute," said Volker.

And indeed, the next time I was back in Canada, I told Der Gute all about this.

"And Volker says he will have a word with you when he comes to visit."

Der Gute shrieked.

"Oh no! I am so worried!"

"Apparently teddy bears are not a universal German-man thing."

"Well, no," admitted Der Gute. "Of course not. But I like

them. And my mother keeps giving them to me. What am I supposed to do?"

Shortly thereafter, Der Gute reported that he'd had to leave his residence in the middle of the night due to a fire alarm.

"Did you take your bear?"

"Well, of course. He would have been furious if I left him."

As it turned out, Volker never had that word with Der Gute. He had a word with me instead, and I found myself telling Der Gute about the break-up. Der Gute was sorry, but one thought was uppermost in his mind.

"Did you tell him more about my teddy bear?"

"No, Der Gute, I did not tell him more about your teddy bear."

"If he does not like teddy bears, he must be weird, really. Stay away from him."

Despite everything, I had to laugh. Der Gute was pleased.

"So does that make me a better husband?" he demanded.

"Maybe," I said. "You certainly make me laugh."

The Age Thing

Der Gute is buying a pet fish today. I heard all about it last night when we met up at a bistro for a drink. It will be red, and he can keep only one of them because otherwise they would fight. I don't know what this says about fish society as a whole, but Der Gute finds it fascinating. He imagined putting two of these fish together to see them do battle. Meanwhile, he has never been allowed to have a fish before, but his mother is in Germany, so Der Gute is free.

In the middle of these ruminations, my friend Red arrived, slipping off from a "drink thing" down the street. She looked like a million bucks in her green and gold halter dress, and she gobbled a cocktail with great enjoyment. Red is an opera singer and Der Gute is musical, so we discussed German opera and songs. I was rapt, but Der Gute kept going off in a dream. I suspect he was thinking about his fish. Then he was obviously distracted by the pickup football game in the dark street behind us; it looked like the kitchen staff was goofing off.

I was a bit nettled. Here I was, introducing him to an operatic redheaded bombshell, and what did he do? Think about football shenanigans and pet fish.

"Sometimes I don't listen to you," admitted Der Gute as he saw me home. "It is because you are like the age of a wife, so that is why. If you were the age of a mother, I guess I would listen to you more. Ha ha."

"Technically," I said, "I am the age of a mother. I'm almost thirteen years older than you, Der Gute."

"Mmph," said Der Gute.

Then we both went into a dream, and I thought of how appalling it would have been to be a mother at almost-thirteen. In the light of day, when my math and memory are better, I see that actually it would have been impossible. But anyway, that was not the point. The point was to deflect

Der Gute's thoughts on wives, for marrying me has been a theme since he got here. His womenfolk had seized upon the news that in Germany we had gone to a concert and some botanical gardens together and put the idea in his head. It is the subject of many of his jokes. Joke it might be, but the theme is so often repeated, I am beginning to fear being seized in Der Guterly arms. This would be tremendously embarrassing for everybody.

The older I get, the fewer the single men my age, so I wonder if I won't end up marrying some whippersnapper in the end. Possibly I will marry one of my students, and there will be a tremendous and entertaining scandal. But I do like nice Catholic men in their twenties. They are full of ideals, and many are very good-looking. The one problem I see is that they are not entirely grown up. It is one thing to dazzle a boy, but there is the danger that when he grows up he will discover that the glamorous older woman he married is, well, just me.

What Do Aunties Do?

I love children. The older I get, the more my eye is drawn to the little people. Sometimes I wonder what my life would be like if I had studied Early-Childhood Education instead of English Literature and Theology. I'd make more money, I'd be surrounded by wee ones, and I'd sound a lot more attractive on Catholic dating websites.

Fortunately, my mom and dad gave me brothers and sisters, and not only is one of those brothers marrying a woman who also likes children, one of my sisters has already had a baby. My nephew is a loud and bold little toddler with a determined chin. He climbs to dizzying heights on slides and rope ladders. When he falls down (not, thank God, from slides and ladders), he doesn't cry. On the other hand, he is terrified of warm water and wept warm tears this weekend when he thought I was going to subject him to it.

So even at two, my nephew is my kind of man. He is brave, energetic and doesn't make grooming a hobby. He cries when someone else has ice cream, but I know quite a few men like this. (As one friend advised me, you have to know what faults you can live with. My ex-boyfriend Volker was enormously cross when the scientist in the office above him won world fame overnight. But his envious sulking was okay with me.) Also admirable in a young man, my nephew appreciates culture. These days I have been reading him children's poetry, a long step forward from picture books, and he is getting it.

My nephew is also showing signs of a rich imagination. On Saturday evening, I took him to a schoolyard, and he made a cake out of the gravel under the climbing frames. "Chocolate cake," he informed me. He offered some to a youth watching us from a bench. "There's my friend," said Pirate. He is at the stage where everyone is his friend. At one point, he went tearing off after a party of bicyclists cutting through the school field.

"My friends!" he yelled.

"Pirate," I said, my voice deepening with repetition. "Pirate. Pie. PIE! PIRATE! Come here. Come here this instant! PIRATE!"

But, after a few hesitant glances back, he ran towards the bicyclists, tearing across the field with surprising agility. Finally, I ran after him. He ran even harder. Two elderly women with a small black dog watched the pursuit with enjoyment. Finally, I caught him and tackled him to the ground. He giggled with joy. As I led him back, hand in hand, he said:

"I'm the gingerbread man."

I wasn't sure what to say.

"Well, I'm your auntie," I said faintly. "And you have to come when I call."

On Sunday he was back at Grandma and Grandpa's house, and I took him to the park. As I pushed him on the swings, I thought about the joys of being an auntie. Ideally, I'd like to be a mother, but being an auntie is pretty good. The role of a mother is clear to me, but I haven't worked out the responsibilities and opportunities of aunthood yet.

"What do aunties do?" I asked Nephew.

"They make nests," he said with great confidence. "They lay eggs."

Nostalgie de la Boue

I have had a busy Saturday night and Sunday. Last night I walked to my sister's house for a vigorous evening of babysitting. In her award-winning book *Woman: An Intimate Geography*, Natalie Angier posits that the reason women live so long after menopause is that multiple women are needed to help with human childcare. (Too often women used to die in childbirth, and the tough ladies whose children had already grown up took charge.) Now, in my case, menopause is some years away, but I must say that I enjoy babysitting my nephew. It makes me feel important and useful. Of course, it also makes me feel tired and impatient, but never mind that for now.

I have no insight into how Pirate feels about his Auntie Dottie, other than a pleasant association with parks. Auntie Dottie is always good for a trip to the park. Of course, Auntie Dottie has her quirks. For example, she refuses to let Pirate eat dinner, or to eat dinner herself, with the television on. Even when the great goddess Dora the Explorer herself is squeaking from the TV set, Auntie Dottie irreverently turns it off. This, of course, makes Pirate howl with dismay, and Auntie Dottie either ignores him or blows bubbles on his tummy until he stops.

That begins our babysitting schedule. The TV is turned off. Pirate howls. There is dinner. Auntie prays grace loudly and slowly. Pirate ignores this, the wee pagan. Auntie eats her dinner with a good appetite. Pirate eats the best parts and, if he thinks there is any, calls for dessert. Mommy gets ready to go out. Auntie, having learned the hard way, gets Pirate out of the house before Mommy leaves. Being strict, Auntie insists that Pirate wears clothes, preferably clean, out of doors. Pirate gets on his tricycle, and Auntie grasps the handle. (The tricycle has a training handle for minders to grasp and steer.) There is a lot of fun at the park, ending when the sun is low in the sky. Then Auntie and Pirate return to the house, Auntie having promised future treats. Next, they watch TV. After that, Auntie reads as few storybooks as she thinks she can get away with. Finally, there is a pitched battle in which Pirate shrieks that he doesn't want to go to bed.

Yesterday there were a few variations in the program. This time, I encouraged Pirate to ask his mother where she was going and when she would be coming back. He reluctantly gave her permission, and he did not demand to know her whereabouts for the rest of the evening. Second, it had rained heavily earlier in the day, and I encouraged Pirate to drive through the puddles. He enjoyed this. And, as a generous favor beyond all expectation, I let him squish around in a large mud puddle.

I wasn't sure if I should be letting Pirate squish around in the mud. It is not something I would care to do myself. And who knew where that mud had been? But as the mud puddle was between a strip of field and a schoolyard playground, I judged that the mud was as pure as mud went.

No pesticides. No dogs. I held Pirate's sandals and watched him march happily back and forth, his feet and legs growing blacker and blacker.

Human happiness is so often caused by simple things. Rarely have I seen happiness like that of my nephew squishing through the mud. He radiated joy. Squish, squish. Unable to contain himself, he squatted down and rubbed his little hands in the black goo. He stood up and looked at his hands with incredulous joy. I stood a little further back and started rethinking my liberal attitude towards mud.

"Wipe them off on the grass," I ordered. "Wipe them off on the grass!"

He wiped them off on the grass, but there was more where that had come from. He leaned over and rubbed his hands through the black mud again. Behind me I heard an elderly couple laughing with glee. Pirate had mud on his legs, his arms, his shorts, his t-shirt, his face and—horrors!—in his mouth. Now, that is where I draw the line. And thus, alas, I felt that I should teach him immediately how to spit.

"Spit!" I cried and spat.

He was delighted and gave it a try. He wasn't very good at it. I thought about parasites and typhoid. But then I remembered reading that we all eat a peck of dirt eventually, so I decided to relax. Still, I didn't want him tricycling through the neighborhood covered in mud.

"Roll down the hill," I ordered.

Pirate was delighted. He lay down, and I pushed him

down the hill. At the bottom, he was no longer quite so muddy. And after some running around, ("But it's not *dark* yet!"), I convinced him to get on his tricycle and pedal home. And when we got there, I explained to him that while it was okay and natural to get dirty outside the house, little boys have to be clean inside the house. And with that, I took the hose to him, and he was again delighted. He assisted in the whole process by taking his clothes off and, clean, prancing nakedly through the door.

I don't remember ever having squished around in the mud. It seems like something you should do when you are three because you won't have too many opportunities to do so when you are older. Either you don't like getting dirty, or you are afraid of botulism, or society frowns upon you. And therefore, hoping that I would be able to get the stains out of his clothes, I just stood beside the mud puddle and was happy for my nephew.

And now I have to go immediately because he is here and he wants to go on the swings. I might not be a mother, but I am certainly an aunt. And with such privileges come responsibilities.

The Facts of
(Married) Life

Dating Versus Courtship

Now, I am more of an expert on how to stay single than on how to get married. If I knew the getting-married secrets, I'd be raking in millions on the lecture circuit. However, I will give the topic of Dating versus Courtship a shot.

My first thought about the difference between Dating and Courtship is that Dating is what I do, and Courtship is what happens to other people. Ha ha! But seriously, folks, if you don't want to be single anymore, just look at my habits and do the opposite. I have been dating since I was fourteen. Now I am thirty-six. I took a break from dating the year I was married (naturally), but I threw myself right back into the dating scene before the ink was dry on my new lease. And that, *mes amis*, was a hideous mistake.

A minister's stepdaughter told me once that divorcing people were at least temporarily insane and not to be dated. I believe that, for I was definitely temporarily insane and squandered my twenties asking out men who did not give two pins for me but were lonely enough to hang out.

Okay, so the first thing to note here is that there is a real difference between dating and courtship. Dating is what people do because they are lonely. Courtship is what people do because one or both are falling in love. And because falling in love is the ideal, people don't marry the people they are just dating.

The sad thing, of course, is that one person might be courting the other, whereas the other thinks they are just dating. And this—alas—I firmly believe is the case when a nice, marriage-positive Catholic woman asks a man out. *She* is courting; *he* is just dating. We persist in believing that men—especially shy men—just need a little boost, and then they will be emboldened to begin courting us. Uh—no. When men fall in love, they begin courting. *They* make that phone call. *They* come up with the lame excuse to begin a conversation. *They* make the invitation to coffee. If a man in love is too darn shy to make that phone call, then he just isn't ready to have an adult relationship.

The other sad thing is that a woman cannot make a man fall in love with her. It's impossible. A man either falls in love with you or he doesn't. But a woman can sometimes be charmed into love. If a man has the guts and brains to do impressive things, figure out what makes his beloved laugh, cleans up his act, attunes his ear to what she wants, and shows heroic fidelity, well, she just might fall in love with him. (Of course, if a man persists in a clumsy, stupid fashion, the woman might become terrified and call the cops. If a woman says, point blank, "Don't call me," don't call her.)

Therefore, I believe that women cannot and should not

directly court men. The most we can do is smile at them and invite them to parties we throw with other girls. In public, we should be the best version of ourselves. And when guys dig us, we should both notice and consider if we might dig them, too.

Many of you may find this just too retro for words. I did, too, when I was fifteen, and my mother was scolding me for telephoning boys. But I'll tell you—I never asked out any of the men who fell in love with me. And none of the boys or men I asked out ever stuck around. None.

I was watching *Harry Potter and the Goblet of Fire* the other night, and it occurred to me that all those modern Wizard teenagers were obeying the old dating and court-ship rules. The boys were trying to pluck up the courage to ask out the girls. The girls were standing in packs, giggling. Harry and his friend Ron wonder how on earth to get a girl alone to ask her out. It's a bit of a challenge.

Ron's brother boldly asks out Angelina in the middle of class, getting her attention by throwing something at her. Easy as pie. Ron is desperate: even Neville has a date. We find out he has asked out Ron's sister Ginny. Ron asks out Hermione; Hermione has already been asked. Harry asks out Cho Chang, who regretfully turns him down because she's already been asked. Ron loses his head and asks Fleur, the sexy foreign student, who sweeps past him. Both Harry and Ron survive their humiliations. Harry, realizing that the Patil twins keep smiling at him, asks them out for himself and Ron. (Note: Harry does this in desperation at the last minute; the Patil girls are thus doomed to a lousy double date. Fortunately, they are rescued by Bulgarian dreamboats.) My goodness, don't the girls at Hogwarts have the confidence to boldly pursue men? What were you thinking, J.K. Rowling?

I think she's thinking human nature. Men need challenges to test their manhood, and rejection is a risk they must take. Women need to stop sacrificing themselves and settling for second best. Rejection by men doesn't spur us on; it scars us. And therefore, I say, don't date. Court or wait for courtship. Pray for the merely lonely, but don't be their temporary consolation prize.

Honor

I had an e-mail from a reader who is contemplating marriage. Included in the e-mail was a copy of the Roman Catholic wedding vows for his diocese, and they are as follows: "I, xxxxx, take you, xxxxx, to be my (husband/wife). I promise to be true to you, in good times and bad, in sickness and in health. I will love you and honor you all the days of my life." The word that interested my reader was "honor." What does honor mean from a Catholic point of view? he asks. Honor is a word that has many meanings and has too often resulted in horrors. My reader wonders if it wouldn't be better to drop the word "honor" from sacred vows.

My correspondent is right, to a certain extent. The concept of honor has meant terrible things: battlefield massacres, the murder of sisters and daughters, genital mutilation, refusal to admit wrong, and all kinds of bloody shenanigans. Too often, honor has meant limiting women's movements and activities. In urban Canada twenty years ago, this meant some girls were not allowed to date. (I knew several of these.) In urban Canada today, this means that some girls are not allowed to go to school. We hear horror stories from Birmingham and Berlin of young women being killed for leaving arranged marriages, for wearing Western clothes, for daring to speak to an English or German boy. So it is no wonder that my correspondent is leery of the word "honor."

The thing is, I am not the best person to ask. I didn't take these vows—mine were out of the *Book of Common Prayer*—but mine were close enough, and I broke 'em. Of course, I was released from them by a diocesan marriage tribunal, but I can still see the rub-out marks on my conscience. I wasn't true, I didn't love him, and I certainly will not honor him all the days of my life. The best I can do for him is to let him live his life unbothered, to never reveal his name and to remember that he was only twenty-four when I left. Twenty-four. That seems so young now.

So, honor. As usual, in all questions of marriage I turn to the example of my parents. My parents are very private people, and their marriage is a bit of a secret, even from their children. Actually, sometimes I think my parents mentally retreated a little from the treasure hoard of children poured into their laps from above. No wonder—we have outnumbered them for decades. But we are not stupid, and we do notice some things. For example, I have never heard my father say an unkind word to my mother. He very well may have—they have known each other for forty years—but I have never witnessed it. Nor have I ever heard my father say an impatient or unkind word about my mother behind her back. And my mother is similarly kind to and about my father. They have *always* shown a unified front toward their children. There was no undermining of each other's authority. Dad was the benevolent yet absolute monarch; Mom was the power-wielding prime minister. Daddy is the head of the household because Mommy says so. Something like that.

So I think that is what it means to honor your spouse. It means that you do not say unkind things to them in front of others. It means that you do not say unkind things about them to others. It means that you keep a veil of privacy over your marriage; it should be a bit of a mystery, even to your children. It means that you do not undercut your spouse's authority over your children, and that you back each other up constantly. You must always be on their side, even if later you comfort the child who has been punished or denied a treat. And believe me, there is no greater security for a child than the knowledge that Mom and Dad truly love and honor one another.

This is honor as a verb, not as the blood-soaked noun it was in the Crimean War and is in Iraq, in Bangladesh, in London, in Berlin. Honor is not something you own, or that others subscribe to you, or that your daughters can take away from you. Honor, to honor, honoring is an activity, a discipline. I imagine it can be difficult at times, but practice, they say, makes perfect. It is possible, and with the grace of the Holy Spirit, all married couples can and will learn to honor each other, even all the days of their lives.

Great Expectations

Sometimes when a friend rhymes off a whole laundry list of what she or he wants in a potential spouse, I interrupt.

"You can only choose two traits."

"Why only two?"

"Because otherwise you're going to screen out the entire human race. You get two."

"Well, I want him to be really nice to me and—"

"No, you get that one for free. Besides that."

"Then you mean I get *three* traits."

"No, you get two traits on top of basic human decency, which includes being really nice to you."

"Well, I want him to be funny and intelligent."

"Funny and intelligent. Got it. "

"And six feet tall or over."

"*Bzzzt.* Sorry. Only two."

"Dagnabit!"

"*Bzzzt!* Sorry!"

What is it that we expect from marriage, anyway? One of my essays has generated some interesting discussions about the "mystical union" of marriage. Call me a mystical moron, but I don't get it. When I think about human experience, I don't picture husbands and wives hand in hand, having celestial experiences of sudden, cosmic, mutual understanding of each other and God. I see a lot of peasants up to their knees in water, harvesting rice together and returning home at the end of the day, dog tired, to get what comfort they can out of dinner and bed.

But leaving aside the sixth of the world that is a Chinese peasant, what about the leisured West? If we get our version of reality from TV, it is obvious what we expect from marriage. We expect marriage to make up for all the deficiencies of our childhoods. We expect someone to listen to all our woes—unlike Mom, who got tired of them—and to understand us completely, unlike Pop, who was rarely around.

We expect spectacular, fantastic, incandescent sex seven days a week. We expect to be richer, that is for sure. We expect two steady paychecks, woo-hoo, or one solid paycheck and a yummy stay-at-home mommy to stretch the grocery budget like Mom used to. But because we are modern, we expect to be much better than Mom and Pop. We won't be so tired at the end of the day. We'll strap any kids to our backs and see the world. And I guess, when we are religious, we expect to be conscious of a deeply meaningful spiritual-erotic connection, the Judeo-Christian answer to tantric yoga.

Me, I'd expect soap. Lots and lots of soap. It is amazing how much soap gets used up in a marriage. I wonder how much of it my mother used before she developed chronic dermatitis? There is soap for scrubbing tubs and sinks. There is soap for the windows. There is soap for the doors. There is soap for the dishes. There is soap for the floors.

There is laundry soap for regular laundry, and there is gentle soap for delicates. There is soap for washing your hands after changing diapers. There is gentle soap for babies. There is Murphy's oil soap for wood floors and furniture. There is soap for the car. There is special soap for carpets. There is a particularly nasty but vigorous soap for toilets.

Nowadays, there is even soap for vegetables.

Whatever else I would expect from marriage, I would definitely expect soap. And mucus because of living in northern countries. And vomit because of food poisoning and flu. And sweaty t-shirts balled up on the floor. Odd socks. Dust. Burned pots. Beef blood. Bills. Butter stains. You see where I going with this.

Don't get me wrong. I don't have low expectations of marriage. One of the reasons I am still single is because I have extremely high expectations of marriage. If married, I would expect a spouse I could respect for at least forty years. Not only that, I would expect my spouse to love ME for at least forty years. Ooh. Now there's a challenge!

Maybe there *is* a mystical union in marriage. Scripture seems to say so, although St. Paul says the teaching of two becoming one flesh is "a great mystery, but I speak in reference to Christ and the church" (Ephesians 5:32). If Scripture says so, that's enough for me. But I wonder if people are conscious of this mystical union? And if they aren't, isn't that just one more overly romantic expectation?

Peer Marriages

Good news for women today. You know, I am tired of so-called scientists telling us that contemporary men behave the way they do because of their caveman ancestors. After all, it is difficult to know what our caveman ancestors actually did, because they didn't leave many records. I believe they liked to paint, make weapons, hunt, fish and bury their dead in a way that suggests they believed in an afterlife. I don't think there's evidence that they were obsessed with spreading their genes around or mating with women with childbearing hips. I mean, come on. I am sure there were devoted husbands thousands of years ago who chose their wives either because they fell in love with their personalities or because their parents said so. The Bible, three thousand years closer to cavemen than we are, is very down on promiscuous baby-having and very up on men sticking with the wives of their youth.

These days many traditional Catholic men want to marry younger women to ensure big families. I find this depressing. I love big families, and I think a big family is the greatest gift

God can give you after himself. However, I am probably not going to have many children myself now, being unmarried at thirty-six. And there are fantastic women out there who are also not going to have many children because of their health, their age or their economic situation. Frankly, if I ever have even one child, I will consider this a great gift and a miracle. But evolutionary psychology says that the older I get, the less likely men will want to have this marvelous baby with me. Sad, eh? But guess what: evolutionary psychology is wrong.

In their *The Spiritual Brain: A Neuroscientist's Case for the Existence of the Soul*, Mario Beauregard and Denyse O'Leary write, "Another evolutionary psychology prediction, that men prefer fertile women who can spread their genes, did not pan out …. In fact men (like women) prefer mates in the same general age group as themselves. The statistics are skewed because most men who are still *seeking* mates are young." This is great news for us older gals, for it occurs to me that unmarried men our age do not really want all those children after all. If they were that interested in having multiple children, they would have had some already.

It could be that the older single men get, the more they want to spend time with an adult companion, not play with children or build families around themselves. As long as they are interested in cultural and intellectual pursuits, like concerts and travel, they and older single women would indeed make good companions for each other. A man with no children who wants a wife just so that he has somebody to keep his bed warm, help with the housework and watch TV with him is lazy and possibly infantile. But an older single man who does not want to be thinking about university tuition when he is sixty-five, but otherwise enjoys the world around him, is a prize.

When I think about this a little more, I realize that we older Catholic women are quite attractive from many points of view. Catholics are often torn between wanting to be faithful to the teachings of *Humanae Vitae* and the economic difficulties of having many children. Older Catholic couples can obey the letter of the law without the fear that they will end up with old-style Quebec-sized families. Also, whereas younger Catholic men may have the energy to argue with multiple disobedient children, I'm guessing older ones don't. In addition, younger women might not know exactly who they are yet. Older women are a take-me-as-I-am proposition. What you see is what you get. There will be fewer dramatic and distressing surprises. And finally, older women find older men attractive, not because they are "older men" but because…Hmm…I don't know, actually. All I can tell you is that I never even noticed a man over forty until I was thirty. Men over forty simply did not exist for me. I couldn't understand why any woman would desire a man who was losing his hair. But then I turned thirty, and suddenly there were cute men over forty all around me.

Wedding Basher

My mother always told us that if something were advertised on TV, we would not get it for Christmas. This led some of us to believe that TV was an evil thing and not to be trusted. Ditto for advertising. Perhaps once upon a time TV shows were separate from the advertising. However, that is no longer true. *Sex and the City*, for example, sells a sexual philosophy, Manolo Blahnik and Jimmy Choo shoes, and New York. *Desperate Housewives*, I'm told, sells La Perla lingerie. But this kind of advertising is new only in its brazenness. For a long time, TV shows have sold weddings. Fancy, expensive weddings.

Twelve years ago, the average Canadian wedding cost ten thousand dollars. I know this because twelve years ago my parents were planning to pay for my wedding. When this price tag was mentioned on the news, they both gasped in horror. My youngest sister found this hilarious and recounted the story over the phone. I didn't find it hilarious. I had enough stress and guilt already. Fortunately, my ill-fated wedding did not cost my parents ten thousand dollars. And my divorce cost me less than a thousand.

It seems absolutely bizarre to me that it costs so much to get married. There is a lovely Norman Rockwell painting that seems to be of a man and woman getting married in a registry office. Once upon a time, the registry office was good enough. And, hey, in Boston, a marriage license costs a mere

$50—"cash only." You don't even have to get a blood test any-more. As for church weddings, which Christians prefer these days, my Protestant grandparents got married in their local church on a Friday afternoon. They wore their best suits and went back to my grandfather's parents' house for sandwiches and lemonade. Then they went by train to Montreal or Que-bec or some barely exotic locale like that. And, surprise, they were married until the day my grandfather died.

My friend Christine and her husband did themselves and everyone else a favor by going to Las Vegas and being married by Elvis. I forget if they threw a party when they got home. I hope so. I imagine it as an informal scene of unbridled cocktail drinking. And I think it is unfair that Catholics can't get away with this. Catholics, who have to get married in church AND give their parish six months' to a year's notice, are almost forced into horrific expense. And because I keep hearing about Catholics who live together because they can't "afford" to get married yet, I think that these instructions are occasions of sin.

So in order to do my bit in the battle of good and evil, I am no longer going to fancy weddings. I am going to boycott all weddings except those of my immediate family and best friends. After all, guests are perfectly expendable. If we refuse to come, the expense of dinner is less. And to be frank, being a guest is not all that much fun when you're single. A wed-ding reception is a blatant negation of the Single Life. The bride and groom are, in effect, saying, "We're in love! We're not single anymore! Whoo-hoo!" Is it any wonder that so many people get completely drunk at wedding receptions? It is the only way they can get through a very boring night.

What I hope is that one day small weddings will come back into fashion. Brides will pick nice smart suits that they can also wear to job interviews. Grooms will book tickets to a nearby honeymoon location. Families will make a lot of sandwiches and some lemonade. Priests will agree to small, short ceremonies on weekday afternoons, without the paternalistic demand of a one-year waiting period. The wedding will be thus truly the beginning, and not the goal, of a marriage.

Mom and Dad: A Love Story

Most of the love stories in my life are pretty trivial. A crush on a blond boy in sixth grade. A crush on a dark-haired boy in—what am I in now?—twenty-third grade. But the one love story that my life and happiness depend upon is the continuing love story of Mom and Dad.

Today is my mom and dad's wedding anniversary. They were married long ago, when my mom was an infant of twenty-three and my dad a stripling of twenty-nine. The camera didn't work well indoors, but we have some great photographs of my parents outside the snow-covered university church where they were married. My mom carried a bouquet of red poinsettias that blazed against her homemade, fur-trimmed white dress. My dad carried a hat that he put on his head as he went out the church door. His car, a Volkswagen Bug, waited by the steps. I love these pictures. My parents look so *cute.*

They are still very cute, only in an older, squishier way, of course. They sit in the parlor, on either side of an antique yellow leather-topped table, reading books and exuding tranquility. My mom is an avid crossword puzzler, so occasionally the companionable silence is broken by her cry of "Italian for *his darling,* four letters!" "*Cara,*" pronounces my dad. "Ah," says my mom. Scribble, scribble. My dad visits my mother every day at tea time at the bookshop where she works. They drink coffee and gaze companionably at the stacks of paperbacks. Books have featured significantly in the love story of Mom and Dad.

It is hard for me to express just how grateful I am that my parents love each other. After all, it gets mixed up in my gratitude for all the other things about them. Everything I have (except my friend Melanie's clothes and my friend Kelly's extra socks) I owe to them. But, after my own merry existence, what I am most grateful to them for is that they gave me my brothers and sisters. Some people hoard their love, and don't want children to "come and wreck everything." Well, the mob of us broke a lot of things—china, windows, hockey sticks, heads—but we never wrecked the love and generosity of Mom and Dad.

Got Your Back

Near the beginning of my book-reviewing career, I was handed a sloppy, badly written and boring volume of theology. It made me so angry that I threw it across the room. I don't know what made me more furious, the heterodoxy, the stale hectoring tone or the gosh-awful clichés. I begged the book editor to free me from this onerous task. But he sternly told me to just write what I thought. So, deciding to leave the bad writing alone, I went after the heterodoxy. After I wrote my skin-peeling review, I discovered that the author was not, as I thought, a non-Catholic amateur. The author was actually a theology professor. I realized then that I could get into trouble. However, I told myself not to be a wimp: if I was prepared to flay some confused greenhorn, I should be prepared to give a professor the same treatment.

The professor went ballistic. Angry e-mail to the paper. Angry e-mail to me through the paper. Angry e-mail to my unpublished university e-mail account. Whew! I was rattled. But the book editor also e-mailed me, and he said something like, "We stand by your book review." In short, "Got your back." Still rattled, I confided my worries to my mentor. My mentor laughed and snorted at the angry e-mail news. "The Empress has no clothes!" he shouted. In short, "Got your back."

Why do older women still want to get married? In the

end, I think, it is because we want someone who will always say, "Got your back," and mean it. This is not a rescue fantasy. Oh sure, some women, very poor and tired women or women who are infantile, want some man to come along and lift them to a wealthier way of life. But my guess is that most women just want a nice man who will be there for them through thick and thin. Sure, we can fight our own battles, but the battle is more easily won with reinforcements. A mother arguing with her child will win a lot sooner if there's a father to back her up. An office worker who comes home exhausted and in tears will be able to put the day behind her better if there's someone at home to say, "They're all idiots. You don't deserve that, honey." A young woman who is being hassled on the street is usually freed from the annoyance when her boyfriend/husband/brother shows up. He's got her back.

The happiness of family life depends a lot on whether we all "get each other's back." Marriages fail when one spouse refuses to back up the other or bear his or her fair share of the load of life. Children are driven to despair when parents cold-shoulder their worst difficulties, or—God forbid—take the part of an abusive spouse or boyfriend. But families flourish when its members go out of their way to be kind to one another. My younger brother bailed me out of a financial mess; I'll never forget that. My other brother tore a strip off an anonymous commenter on my blog; I'll never forget that, either. My youngest sister didn't run the last time I sat on the kitchen floor and cried. (I am the only adult public weeper in the family.) She didn't know what to say, but she didn't run. That was years ago, but I haven't forgotten.

Yes, I guess like so many women, I do hanker after the knight on the charging horse to rescue me from the dragons. Of course, the image I prefer is of me fighting the dragon by myself, and not doing a bad old job of it, when my handsome comrade-in-arms shows up to help. But in reality, I've got some friends and family on their metaphorical chargers, so all is well. They've got my back.

✳ Acknowledgments

In writing this book, I have drawn water from many wells. First was the incomparable *Live Alone and Like It* by Marjorie Hillis Roulston. Then was the celebrated *The Rules: Time-tested Secrets for Capturing the Heart of Mr. Right* by Ellen Fein and Sherrie Schneider, a book I simultaneously embraced and resisted. There was also *The Girls' Guide to Surviving a Break-up* by Delphine Hirsh. Moving from the heart to the head, I admit to reading Natalie Angier's *Woman: An Intimate Geography* and *The Spiritual Brain: A Neuroscientist's Case for the Existence of the Soul* by Mario Beauregard and Denyse O'Leary. Finally, I cannot deny a debt to Bernard Lonergan's *Insight: A Study of Human Understanding* and confess a hope that my comparatively slender work will win a place on the shelves of Toronto's Lonergan Research Institute.

This book grew out of two years of writing on my blog, Seraphic Singles. I have scores of readers whom I should like to thank, but first among them are those who appear as characters in this book, some allowing their own proper names to appear and some quite understandably preferring pseudonymity. Thus I would like to thank Volker Zwei, Boston Girl, Jonathan, Tedmund, McKelvie, Lily, Melanie, Kelly, Red, Der Gute, and the Cummings family. Further thanks are owed to Dawn Eden, Weronika Hansen, Lise Legault, Tricia Postle, Simon Schade, and Michael Swan. I am grateful also to Joseph Sinasac and Anne Louise Mahoney of Novalis.

Finally, I would like to thank Mark McLean for his support in the final stages of this manuscript. Got your back.